"The Tracys have done all of us a great service with this wise and tender book. They themselves have worked for years to achieve a healthy intimacy in their own marriage and their reflections are of benefit to everyone. Steve and Celestia are godly, caring, sensitive people who have worked through these issues over decades. Their own marriage is a mature one, tempered by suffering, and marked by devotion to God and one another. The book is a treasure trove, earthy, real, heavenly, delightful. Expect to be blessed and enriched in your own relationships."

—William David Spencer
Ranked Adj. Professor of Theology and the Arts
Gordon-Conwell Theological Seminary

"Here Steve and Celestia show by conviction, research, and experience that for a couple to know one another, at any level, requires wisdom. The insight they offer from many sources of counsel will be a helpful eye-opener for those of us who have assumed way too much about what it really means to care for one another."

—Mart De Haan
President
RBC Ministries

Forever and Always

The House of Prisca and Aquila

Forever and Always

The Art of Intimacy

CELESTIA G. *and* STEVEN R. TRACY

WIPF *&* STOCK · Eugene, Oregon

FOREVER AND ALWAYS
The Art of Intimacy

Wipf & Stock
An Imprint of Wipf and Stock Publishers
199 W. 8th Ave., Suite 3
Eugene, OR 97401

www. wipfandstock.com

ISBN 13: 978-1-60608-960-6

Manufactured in the U.S.A.

To Celestia, my most cherished friend, lover, and ministry partner for over thirty years. How could we, as two starry-eyed kids, have imagined what God was to do in and through our relationship? You are God's greatest earthly gift to me. You are the best intimacy coach a husband could dream of. You make my life a grand, joyful, faith-stretching adventure!

An excellent wife, who can find? For her worth is far above jewels. . . .
Strength and dignity are her clothing,
And she smiles at the future. She opens her mouth in wisdom,
And the teaching of kindness is on her tongue.

Proverbs 31:10, 25–26

To Steven, my faithful husband, the father of our three children, my sheltering tree. You are the most exquisite gift God has given me. I have grown strong in your love and, because of you, know more deeply the love of God.

Husbands, love your wives as Christ loved the church
And gave himself up for her,
That he might present the church to himself in splendor,
Without spot or wrinkle or any such thing,
That she might be holy and without blemish.
In the same way, husbands should love their wives as their own bodies.

Ephesians 5:25–28

To my father, our father, Tom Tracy, who passed away during the writing of this manuscript. You lived before me the clearest model of steadfast marital love for over half a century. Many of the intimacy insights reflected in this book have come from your words and example.

Contents

Acknowledgments

WHILE A BOOK REFLECTS the words of its author(s), these words are shaped and influenced by the individuals who have gone before. Our parents gave us our earliest impressions of everlasting love. Together they celebrate more than 100 years of marital devotion and faithfulness to promises made. Very few enjoy the legacy of enduring love that we have been given. We are sobered by our responsibility to share what we have received with others along the way.

James VanFossan, you are an anointed artist and ministry partner of many years. You entered this project as a single man and have since reaped the fruit of intimacy in your life. Today, you are married to the woman of your dreams and have welcomed Sophia, your firstborn child, into this world. Thank you, James, for sharing your exquisite gift of art to those who have no words. You fill in the spaces.

Bill Spencer and Deb Beatty Mel, you patiently read and edited our first manuscript—adding your comments to guide and protect along the way. Your love was evident throughout this first draft, and we thank you for your kind help. And to the folks at Wipf and Stock Publishers and Patrick Harrison, who painstakingly prepared this manuscript for publication, we thank you.

We thank our humble and godly leaders at Mending the Soul Ministries. You have given us most helpful feedback, prayer, and encouragement. Janet Martin, Peggy Bilsten, Roxane Thorstad, Dan Hoffman, Peter Kinkle, Christine Stephenson, Dagny and Shawn Mallory, Mike and Beth Rehm, Jody and Jeanie Humber, and many others have believed not only in us, but also in God's power to heal brokenness and restore intimacy in each of our lives. You are our community of love, and we grow in your presence. We have worked shoulder to shoulder, helping the broken find healing in Jesus' name.

Our colleagues at Phoenix Seminary graciously granted a research leave so that I would have time to properly focus on this manuscript. We thank you. Our partners in Africa have given us unprecedented examples of selfless love for others and for Christ. Our daughter Abby has devoted her young life to serving the poorest of the poor in the slums of Kampala, Uganda. You have shown us the power of God's fierce, persistent love to reach into the darkest places to redeem the marginalized and the hopeless. Our incredible colleagues at Global Training Network have provided indispensible financial and prayer support as we wrote this manuscript. We thank God for the amazing circle of friends and family he has given us. Each of you continue to touch and shape our concepts of intimacy.

Bill and Aida Spencer, our colleagues at Gordon-Conwell Theological Seminary believed in this project from its inception. Thank you for walking alongside us and for living an ethic of promises kept that has produced more than thirty-five years of committed love. You have given us voice. You are more than ministry partners; you are friends.

And finally, we thank our precious children; three by birth and two by marriage, who patiently walked alongside us in the process of creating and writing. You listened, shared ideas, encouraged, prayed, and allowed absences for this book. We are most blessed by your love and share this work with you. You are our joy.

Two are better than one, because they have a good reward for their toil.
For if they fall, one will lift up the other;
But woe to one who is alone and falls
and does not have another to help. . . .
And though one might prevail against another,
Two will withstand one.
A threefold cord is not quickly broken.

Ecclesiastes 4:9–10, 12 (NRS)

Introduction

Christ kisses us into wholeness through each other.

—Philip Newell

THIS BOOK IS A primer for becoming close to someone. It is a handbook for understanding the stages involved in bonding or attaching closely to another human being. Marriage, the most intimate of all human relationships, is described in Scripture as a "one-flesh mystery" (Eph 5:31–32). This mystery of human bonding is as beautiful as it is complex, particularly in a post-Eden world. Our ability to create intimate relationships as adults is a more natural process if we have enjoyed earlier experiences of safe and nurturing comfort. However, those of us who have not experienced relationships of health, safety, and security often find we need roadmaps along the way. Many of us are woefully aware of our own relational deficits, yet lack vibrant marriages around us to emulate. If you are among the many who have experienced painful and frustrating adult relationships that have shaken your confidence, this book is for you. Our desire is that in these pages you find personal encouragement and direction that is both biblically clear and practical for your relational journey. May you find hope, help, and renewed confidence in marriage. May you increasingly experience the dynamic intimacy that God intends for a man and woman to enjoy—a love for a lifetime.

When we think of facing the raw truth of our relationships, Paul gives us a very encouraging promise: To the degree that we have been wounded and hurt, to that same degree we can know Christ's presence and healing, and to that same degree we can embrace and know real intimacy.[1] We can boldly claim this truth in our significant relationships.

---

1. "Blessed be the God and Father of our Lord Jesus Christ, the Father of mercies and God of all comfort, who comforts us in all our affliction, so that we may be able to

In other words, because of the healing Christ promises, there is no
such thing as being "too damaged to love again." Our intimacy model
is built upon God's bold promises to heal and redeem. His pathways
bring life. He is the only true lover of our souls. Our intimacy with him
is foundational to all other relationships. The Hebrew prophet Hosea
beautifully describes God's love and relentless pursuit of us in order to
heal us and draw our hearts back to himself. He is our first and truest
lover. He states:

> Therefore, behold, I will allure her, and bring her into the wil-
> derness, and speak tenderly to her. And there I will give her her
> vineyards, and make the Valley of Achor a door of hope. . . . And
> in that day, says the LORD, you will call me, "My husband," and
> no longer will you call me, "My Baal." . . . And I will betroth you
> to me forever; I will betroth you to me in righteousness and in
> justice, in steadfast love, and in mercy. I will betroth you to me in
> faithfulness; and you shall know the LORD.[2]

God is delighted when we delight in his love. As a counselor, I
(Celestia) am privileged to participate in the fascinating and individu-
alized process of God making himself known to each one who comes
honestly and humbly to him. This "embossing" of God's love upon our
heart and soul serves as the foundation from which we begin to intimately know another. Only when we come to God honestly in our brokenness and receive his anointing touch that redeems our sense of value
and worth can we boldly and unselfishly approach another human being
with the same vulnerable, life-giving love and forgiveness that we have
received.

J. Philip Newell reminds us to not limit or exclusively define
ourselves by our failures and struggles. Rather, a proper and balanced
understanding of human nature comes from understanding who God
has created us to be—men and women who mirror his beautiful image.
He writes:

> We often define ourselves in terms of the ugliness of what we
> have done or become rather than in terms of the essence of our
> life. We are made in the image of God, in the image of the One
> who is Beauty. Think of a beautiful plant suffering from blight. If

comfort those who are in any affliction, with the comfort with which we ourselves are
comforted by God" (2 Cor 2:3–4).

2. Hos 2:14–20.

botanists were shown such a plant, even if they had never seen that particular type of plant before, they would define it in terms of its essential features and life-force. They would not define it in terms of its blight. Rather, the blight would be described as foreign to the plant, as attacking its essence. This may seem an obvious point botanically, but perhaps it is such an obvious point that we have missed the point when it comes to defining what is deepest within us. In our Western Christian tradition, we have tended to understand human nature in terms of its blight. . . . What is deepest in us is the beauty of our origins. The Scriptures refer to God as the King of beauty. Our origins are in God. We are sons and daughters of beauty, or as the Celtic tradition of fairy tale imagines, we are princes and princesses of beauty.[3]

We were made in and for Eden, but clearly do not live in Eden. Instead, we bump around in a dusty and relationally fractured world. Our souls long for the very intimacy we are created for, but rarely experience. In many ways, our eyes have become dulled to the beauty in ourselves and in those around us. Seeing, we don't really see anymore.

A nondescript young man stood against the smudged wall of the Washington, DC, metro, L'Enfant Plaza Station. He wore a tattered T-shirt and white jeans. A baseball cap was pitched nonchalantly upon his head. He played an old violin taken from a plain case left open and turned toward the pedestrian traffic. It was a dingy setting and bitterly cold. He played a selection of six classical pieces for approximately forty-three minutes. It was rush hour, and roughly 1,100 people pushed through the metro during that time on their way to work. The acoustics were kind to this young musician and bounced the notes back rich and resonant. The young violinist played for more than three minutes before anyone noticed or dropped a coin in the box at his feet. In fact, the first one to pay any attention at all was a three-year-old little boy. He tried to stop and listen to the music while his mother impatiently pulled his arm, requiring him to maintain her pace. The child continued to cock his head, straining to see and listen. Curiously, children were the ones who

---

3. Newell, *Echo of the Soul,* 60. We certainly do not deny the doctrines of original sin and pervasive human depravity (cf. Rom 3:9–23; 5:12–21). Unfortunately, Newell is ambiguous on this point. Newell correctly notes, however, that we cannot understand human beings correctly by merely looking at the "sinful blight" in fallen humans. Rather, we must look at the original human creation to understand what God intended for human beings. As we will see in the following chapter, even fallen humans are still made in God's image and must be viewed as such (Gen 9:6; Jas 3:9).

showed the most interest, but, without exception, were rushed through by harried parents. During the forty-three minutes the violinist played, only seven people paused to listen, and just a handful gave money. The musician collected only $32.17 for his performance. When the music stopped, no one noticed. Silence reigned until a lone listener meekly applauded.

The metro musician that day was Joshua Bell, one of the world's most skilled and famous classical violinists. He had played six exceedingly difficult pieces by Johann Bach on a Stradivarius violin valued at $3.5 million. In another setting, Bell's musical performance would command $1,000 per minute. Hours after being ignominiously received by his subway audience, Bell traveled to Europe, where he played in packed auditoriums to adoring fans. Then, he returned to the United States to accept the Avery Fisher Prize, recognizing him as the best classical musician in America.

What prompted this bizarre subway performance? On January 12, 2007, Gene Weingarten of the *Washington Post* conducted a provocative social experiment about people's perceptions of beauty by hiring Bell to play the same pieces in the subway that he had played days before to a sold-out Bostonian audience who paid roughly one hundred dollars apiece to hear him perform. In an interesting interview with the violinist the afternoon of the experiment, Bell surprisingly admitted feeling nervous and cautious about performing in the Washington metro. Mind you, Bell had played to the most distinguished audiences around the world—crowned heads of Europe and countless other dignitaries. However, he explained his unexpected feelings of anxiety and uncertainty by saying, "When you play for ticket-holders, you are already validated. I have no sense that I need to be accepted. I'm already accepted. Here, there was this thought: 'What if they don't like me? What if they resent my presence?'" Weingarten summarized Bell's experience as "art without a frame."[4]

The journalist also described interviewing many of the distracted people who had rushed by the master violinist. One of them was a labor contract attorney named Jackie. When asked if she had heard the violinist in the subway, Jackie said she had, but wasn't impressed: "Nothing about him struck me as much of anything." Jackie admitted that she wasn't really listening to the music: "I was just trying to figure out what he was

4. Weingarten, "Pearls Before Breakfast."

doing there, how does this work for him, can he make much money. . . .
I was analyzing it financially."[5] Many of the subway travelers who walked
by while Bell played were listening to personal music players or talking on their cell phones. As an example, when Weingarten interviewed
Calvin Myint several hours after the subway performance, Calvin had
no memory of a musician being anywhere in sight. How could that be?
Calvin was plugged into an MP3 player, listening to "Just Like Heaven."
Ironically, this song was written by a British rock band called The Cure,
and is about a man who has found the woman of his dreams, but cannot
express his love for her until she is gone. "It's about failing to see the
beauty of what's plainly in front of your eyes."[6]

We would also suggest it is about not risking the expression of
your appreciation and love for the beauty that is before you. It seems
the explosion of technology has perversely limited, and not expanded,
our appreciation of new experiences. It has diminished, not enhanced,
our ability to perceive the real beauty that is in and around us. We have
replaced seeing and adoring beauty, both in the God who loves us and
in the people around us, with a frantic drive to work and accumulate
wealth. This trade has left us very poor indeed.

We are to be the frame for the divine "art" in our spouse. Lewis
Smedes, in his compelling fable on forgiveness and marriage, speaks of
"magic eyes" and their power to transform a wretched relationship. He
describes the redemptive power of unconditional, intentional love and
forgiveness by one spouse to another.[7] You see, forgiveness and love are
bound together. One cannot experience one without the other. There is
only one remedy for the ache of a broken heart, and that is the healing
power of forgiveness. When someone has hurt us, forgiveness frees us to
experience that person in a new light. God is able to turn back the pain
and release our hearts to humbly love again. God uses his "magic eyes"
with us and gives us the ability, if we choose it, to see the "magic" or the
"shining" in those around us. The miracle of this is that, as you see the
one you love with God's eyes, beauty is activated and brought to life like
it has never been before. Your beloved will perceive herself differently
because of the love she has received from you. The love in your eyes
will reflect back to her an image of herself that she has not experienced

5. Ibid.

6. Ibid.

7. Smedes, *Forgive and Forget*, xvii–xviii.

before. What a concept! A relational wand is placed in your hands. What you see you can appreciate, and what you appreciate you can praise, and what you praise you can activate; it literally comes to be.

> When we forgive, we come as close as any human being can to the essentially divine act of creation. For we create a new beginning out of past pain that never had a right to exist in the first place. We create healing for the future by changing a past that had no possibility in it for anything but sickness and death. When we forgive we ride the crest of love's cosmic wave; we walk in stride with God.[8]

We have the opportunity—no, the responsibility—to look until we *see* the unique design in the one before us. We are to be the relational "frame" for God's art in each other, to showcase the beauty that we see. We can draw out this hidden beauty in each other by serving one another with a joy-filled, Christlike love. In fact, Scripture dares us to do so—pouring our lives out for each other: "*We know love by this, that he laid down his life for us—and we ought to lay down our lives for one another.*"[9] It is a curious thing that God has created us so that we can feel and believe in our value and worth when we are treated with value and worth. And when we are treated with value and worth, we then can offer that same kind of valuing love to others. This is the "responsibility of love"[10] that we each carry for the people God puts in our lives—but especially for our spouse.

So together, let's slow down and actually learn how to "love, not [just] in word or speech, but in truth and action."[11] Let's learn to offer *presence* as a sacred gift to one another so that we can be made more holy by our sacrifices of love. John assures us that there "is no fear in love, but perfect love casts out fear ... and whoever fears has not reached perfection in love. We love because he first loved us."[12] Let us trust God for

---

8. Ibid., 152.

9. 1 John 3:16.

10. We read this phrase first in our daughter Abigail's blog. She lives and works full time with street children in the slums of Kampala, Uganda. Her stories and photos of living out this "responsibility of love" to children who literally have been thrown away can be found at http//Africa-love.livejournal.com.

11. 1 John 3:18.

12. 1 John 4:18–19.

his pathways of intimacy, and then eagerly anticipate his transforming power in your relationships—with him and each other.

What must we take with us for this journey of intimacy? Faith. Not faith in ourselves or our abilities, but faith in the one who created us so that we can take the sacrificial and vulnerable steps love requires. Walter Wangerin tells of a time when, as a very young child, he was put by his father on a train bound from Chicago to Grand Rapids. He was terrified to "be thrust alone into the dark tunnel of the future."[13] As a child, if he had his way, he would never have left home, his only known safe haven. At that time, his father's only reassurance was to say, "I am going ahead of you. Do you think I would leave you alone? I'll meet you at the station in Grand Rapids. Wait, wait, and see if I don't."[14] He was comforted and set free to travel. He did not have the knowledge of *how* his father would be there, but he had the *promise* of his father—the one who loved him. And so do we.

> *The God of all grace,*
> *Who has called you to his eternal glory in Christ,*
> *will himself restore, support, strengthen, and establish you.*
> *To him be the power forever and ever.*[15]

---

13. Wangerin, *As for Me and My House*, 24.
14. Ibid.
15. 1 Pet 5:10–11.

PART ONE

Foundations of Intimacy

Once Upon a Time

1

God's Original Design

> Just as we are more than the bodies we can see, we are more than
> our individual, separate selves. . . . We literally do not know who
> we are apart from our relationship with others.
>
> —David P. Gushee[1]

W E GREW UP IN the Valley of the Sun (Phoenix) and cavorted away
countless childhood afternoons swimming in backyard pools
with friends. For the boys in my (Steve's) neighborhood, that typically
involved riotous games of keep-away with tattered rubber balls. Decades
later, I still vividly recall catching the prize in the deep end of the pool,
instantly being mugged by a feral prepubescent pack of boys, and being held under water until I released the ball. Sometimes even after
coughing up the oval prize, there were so many flailing bodies on top of
me that I couldn't reach the surface. In mere seconds I would begin to
panic—lunging, punching, and kicking my way to the surface. As much
as I wanted to win, wanted to swim, and wanted friends, oxygen was my
essential need!

CONNECT OR DIE: THE BIOLOGY OF HUMAN INTIMACY

What about human intimacy? Most of us want social interaction. All but
the most reclusive hermit eventually feel lonely and want to be around
others. We want and enjoy friendships. But is intimacy essential? Is it as
vital as oxygen? In a word, yes! Obviously, relational deprivation does
not affect us as quickly and dramatically as oxygen deprivation, yet it
is no less essential for emotional and spiritual health. Sometimes, it is

1. Gushee, *Only Human*, 58, 63.

essential for life itself. From birth, humans need relational contact. For instance, infants who are given basic care but little or no physical touch and human interaction literally can fail to thrive and eventually die. Our understanding of the life-sustaining importance of touch was advanced immediately after World War II when relief organizations were overwhelmed with thousands of orphaned infants. The babies' physical needs were met, but workers had little time to hold or interact with the children. Before long, large numbers of infants became listless, failing to thrive, and many died. Mortality rates among these orphans rose so sharply that authorities were called in to conduct tests to see if there was some contagious disease spreading among the children. After a careful assessment, it was determined that there was no disease or other physical etiology causing these deaths. Rather, the children were failing to thrive because they needed human contact. Once grandmothers were brought in to the orphanages simply to rock and hold the infants, mortality rates plummeted. A few decades later, a similar phenomenon was observed with orphans in Romania. These children were often packed into drab rooms where they received little human contact or physical touch. Caregivers were responsible for up to thirty children each. These children's social deprivation caused many of them to engage in disturbing self-soothing actions such as head banging, incessant rocking, and hand flapping. Many of the children began to waste away physically and mentally. Furthermore, even when they were later adopted into stable, loving homes outside Romania, many of these children continued to exhibit profound social, cognitive, and emotional problems that were largely nonexistent among noninstitutionalized Romanian children.[2]

Recent scientific research has given us deeper biological insights into why and how human connection is essential for physical and emotional health. In the mid 1990s, researchers such as Dr. Bruce Perry conducted neuroscientific and clinical research on child maltreatment, which led to significant discoveries regarding the anatomical impact of neglect on young children. Through the use of MRIs and other research tools, Perry demonstrated that social deprivation, particularly from caregivers, alters young children's brains in such a way as to disturb development. Neglect creates long-term, sometimes severe, neurological impairment in various areas of the brain, particularly those that regulate emotion and impulse

2. Fisher et al., "Problems Reported by Parents"; Kaler and Freeman, "Analysis of Environmental Deprivation."

control.[3] In other words, extreme neglect, often termed "global neglect," can cause physiological brain damage. Severely neglected children have regions of their brains that are significantly underdeveloped, and these neurological abnormalities can be permanent.[4]

We can understand the profound damage of neglect by briefly explaining brain development. The human brain is one of our largest organs, weighing three and a half pounds in the average adult. It is also the most undifferentiated, or undeveloped, organ in the body at birth. There are approximately 100 billion neurons in the human brain, and most of them are present at birth. Human infants' brains do not need additional numbers of nerve cells. In fact, an infant's developing brain has more neurons than it can use and is in the continual process of "pruning," eliminating neurons that are not utilized. The neurons that survive are the ones that become electrically active because synapses have developed, allowing electrical signals to be transmitted. Thus, the human brain is highly "use-dependent" for its development. God in his wisdom wired the human brain so that one of the primary mechanisms that stimulate this process of brain development is *human connection*. More specifically, caregivers' interaction with a baby through touch, facial gestures, verbal reactions, and other responses stimulate the development of synapses, the neuronal pathways that connect the various parts of the brain.[5] Human interaction with infants and children also stimulates subsequent brain development. Some essential skills, particularly language acquisition and proficiency, can only be acquired if there is adequate human interaction during the critical period of brain development from birth to the onset of puberty.[6] In other words, human connection is so essential that, if a perfectly normal, healthy child is deprived of human contact for extended critical periods during childhood, he or she most likely will never be able to develop normal language skills.

We can also understand the critical role relationships play in early human development in terms of healthy *attachment*. Since the

3. Perry and Pollard, "Altered Brain Development"; see also. Chugani et al., "Local Brain Functional Activity."

4. De Bellis, "The Psychobiology of Neglect"; Teicher et al., "Childhood Neglect."

5. Cozolino, *The Neuroscience of Human Relationships,* 84–85; Linden, *The Accidental Mind,* 72–81.

6. For an excellent case study of the impact of severe neglect on brain development and language acquisition, see Rymer, *Genie.*

mid-twentieth century, a great amount of research has gone into understanding long-term human development and emotional wellbeing in terms of the quality of attachment children experience with their primary caregivers, particularly in the first several years of life. There is now an overwhelming consensus among social scientists that the type and quality of relationships children experience, particularly with their primary caregivers, lays the foundation for emotional and relational wellbeing for the rest of a child's life.[7] Sadly, there is also a strong consensus that many of the most socially unhealthy and destructive conditions, such as borderline and antisocial personality disorders, narcissism, and sociopathy, often have their roots in painful, disrupted, and dysfunctional relationships with childhood caregivers.[8] Since more than three-fourths of a child's brain is formed by age three, and early human attachments are most influential, healthy relationships truly impact and shape us for life.

The good news is that we have the opportunity to reverse many of these early social and neurobiological effects upon the brain by creating intimate connections in our adult relationships. A leading neurobiologist explains this dynamic in encouraging physiological terms, noting that we now realize "the brain is capable of change at any time and that social interactions are a primary source of brain regulation, growth, and health. . . . [A]ny meaningful relationship can reactivate neuroplastic processes and actually change the structure of the brain."[9] Amazingly, we can positively shape each other at the deepest level of our hearts, souls, and even our minds. God has given us the privilege and ability to offer deep "repair" to each other through the medium of relationships. We have observed numerous couples who have been deeply wounded in childhood who as adults experience remarkable healing through healthy relationships. In summary, nourishing relationships have tremendous power to stimulate growth and healing in adult contexts.[10] Relational connection is an essential human need.

7. An excellent overview of attachment research is given by Karen, *Becoming Attached.*

8. Beauchaine et al., "Multifinality"; Cozolino, *The Neuroscience of Psychotherapy,* 217–34; Lykken, "The Causes and Costs of Crime."

9. Cozolino, *The Neuroscience of Human Relationships,* 8.

10. Johnson, Browne, and Hamilton-Giachritsis, "Young Children in Institutional Care."

A THEOLOGY OF HUMAN INTIMACY

As Christians, we believe that God uniquely and purposefully created us; we are not the result of blind chance. Furthermore, Scripture gives us rich teaching on human creation and intimate relationships. So, at this juncture, we might ask, Does Scripture teach that intimacy is essential to being human? Why did God "wire" us for relationships?

Creation: All Is Good Unless Alone

The biblical account of God's creation of the universe and all life, including humans, is tantalizingly brief. Often, when I (Steve) lecture in seminary classes on creation, students fixate on what the text does not clearly address. They want to know when Satan fell, how long Adam and Eve were in the garden, and how they lived before the fall. I appreciate inquisitive minds—however, we must not allow the gaps and terse descriptions of the passage to obscure the big, bold picture. A careful reading of Genesis 1 to 3 clearly reveals three fundamental, interconnected truths regarding the original creation:

1. *The original creation was a beautiful divine work that reflected God's very character,* including his goodness, holiness, and power. Throughout the creation process—in fact, six times—God assessed his work as "good" or "very good." We see God's holiness in his creation of a physically and morally perfect garden into which he placed two morally pure and innocent human beings. Sin did not enter the garden of Eden until Genesis 3, when Satan seduced Adam and Eve to eat the forbidden fruit. Furthermore, God's character, unleashed in his unbridled power, is seen dramatically in Genesis 1 where ten times we read "God said," in the context of his power to create instantly and perfectly.[11]

2. *Human beings are the unique apex of all creation; they alone are made in God's image.* Only after God created Adam and Eve did he pronounce his work "very good" (1:31).

11. Wenham notes that "God said" is a common formula in the Hebrew Scriptures, where the reader repeatedly learns that God's word is creative and efficacious. But here in Gen 1, this phrase is used "in a more pregnant sense than usual," for in the creation account these qualities [power, potency, and efficacy] of God's word "are even more apparent" (*Genesis 1–15*, 17–18). The pregnancy of the formula "God said" in Gen 1 to emphasize God's power is highlighted by the six times the formula is followed with "and it was so" (1:7, 9, 11, 14, 24, 30).

3. *God made humans for intimate relationship.* He made a man
   and a woman and gave them to each other to enjoy one-flesh
   intimacy. It is quite significant that, in the entire creation account, the only indication that there was anything lacking in
   this perfect, good creation is when God himself declared, "It is
   not good that the man should be alone; I will make him a helper
   as his partner" (2:18). Humans were not made for isolation, but
   for intimacy![12]

We can tie these three truths together by examining the language
of human creation in Genesis 1:26–28. We read, "Then God said, 'Let
us make humankind in our image, according to our likeness; and let
them have dominion.' . . . So God created humankind in his image, in
the image of God he created him; male and female he created them. God
blessed them, and God said to them, 'Be fruitful and multiply'" (NRSV).
This most essential quality of humans—being made in God's image—is
not defined, but asserted. The Hebrew terms used here for *image* and
likeness are overlapping, nearly synonymous terms that respectively convey *concrete similarity,* as that seen in a statue in someone's precise image
(Dan 3:1), and *abstract similarity,* as seen in something that essentially
looks like something else (Dan 10:16). In other words, we uniquely mirror God. We uniquely reflect his person and character, just as Adam's
son Seth was in Adam's image and likeness, visibly reflecting Adam (Gen
5:3). Christian theologians historically have understood the human
"image of God" in a variety of ways, including the possession of unique
innate abilities such as rationality, power, and authority over creation
("dominion"), and Godlike character qualities (cp. Col 1:15).[13] No doubt,
all of these understandings of "image of God" are correct, for being made
in God's image refers to the myriad of ways we reflect God.[14]

Recently, many biblical scholars have stressed *relationality* as an
essential aspect of the image of God.[15] In other words, being made in

---

12. While Gen 2:18–23 certainly affirms marriage as a beautiful divine gift, it should
not be understood to teach that there was something inherently defective in Adam as an
individual single man, or that there is something defective in a single adult today. The
primary lesson is that humans are made for community. Gossai, "Divine Evaluation."

13. On of the best surveys of historical Christian views of *imago dei* is given by
Stanley J. Grenz, *The Social God and the Relational Self,* 141–82.

14. Hoekema, *Created in God's Image,* 66–73.

15. Grenz, "Theological Foundations for Male-Female Relationships." Karl Barth

God's image means we have a unique, divine-like capacity and mandate for experiencing intimate relationships. Human relationality reflects the fact that God himself is an intrinsically and majestically relational being. The details of Genesis 1:26–28 as well as the broader creation account strongly support this. First of all, in creating us, God describes himself using the plural pronouns "us" and "our." Exegetically, this is best understood as a reference to his relational "divine fullness."[16] God is neither alone nor lonely in his own being because he is in intimate relationship within himself. We know from the fuller revelation of Scripture that, while there is only one God, he exists as three persons: Father, Son, and Holy Spirit. Thus, when God creates in his own image, he creates "male and female": "God is no plain, undifferentiated monad, but living and active, dynamic and personal, so is humankind; we are made for harmonious relationship."[17]

Gender is foundational to being made in God's image, not because God has gender, but because it differentiates us in such a way as to create the capacity and drive for relational intimacy. This is expressed most concretely and powerfully through the act of sexual union, which gives us the power to create life in the image of God. It is noteworthy that the first command God gave Adam and Eve after creating them in his image was to "be fruitful and multiply" (Gen 1:28). In Eden, God sanctions and even mandates marital sex, not just as a physical act, but as an imaging of a larger divine reality. Human sexuality mirrors God by the way it drives us toward relational intimacy: "Sexuality is the human drive toward intimate communion. Beyond the glandular impulse, the human

---

has been particularly influential in making relationality a cardinal element of *imago dei*. For instance, see his *Church Dogmatics*, vol. 3, 183–212. In a major recent work on *imago dei* in the creation account, J. Richard Middleton argues that it is solely functional or missional and refers to humans having a royal calling of acting as God's representatives in earth. Middleton criticizes Barth's relational interpretation of Gen 1:26–28, but concedes that there is some exegetical support for the relational view in light of New Testament teaching (*The Liberating Image*, 21–22). It appears to us that, in developing his thesis, Middleton has relied too heavily on ancient Near Eastern texts, relied too little on the details of the biblical text of Gen 1–2, and has failed to account for other biblical teachings, particularly those which assert that *imago dei* is an intrinsic endowment that all humans possess (cf. Gen 9:6; Jas 3:9), not just a hypothetical potentiality or desirable activity which surely not all humans carry out.

16. Clines, "The Image of God in Man," 62–69; Davidson, *Flame of Yahweh*, 36–42; Hasel, "The Meaning of 'Let Us' in Gn 1:26," 58–66.

17. Sherlock, *The Doctrine of Humanity*, 35.

sexual urge is always toward another person. We want to experience the other, to trust the other and be trusted by him, to enter the other's life by entering the vital embrace of his/her body."[18]

The concluding sentence of Genesis chapter 2 summarizes the creation account in dramatically intimate language. Ironically, while this is the clearest biblical picture of unblemished human intimacy, it is the final one. For the first and only time in history, two human beings experienced nothing but unbroken, perfect oneness as they stood in each other's presence. We read, "The man and his wife were both naked, and were not ashamed" (Gen 2:25). This is one of the only instances in all the Hebrew Scriptures where the term "nakedness" is positive and not associated with some form of humiliation.[19] Throughout the rest of human history, humans have put tremendous energy into hiding and not exposing their real selves, for exposure causes shame. This first human couple stood naked before each other without the slightest stirring of shame. The verbal form of the Hebrew word for "shame" emphasizes both the unbroken duration and the depth of their intimacy. Their shame-free response to each other was not a "single moment of discovery," but instead reflected all they had experienced with each other from the very first moment of creation as they stood completely and reciprocally naked "before each other."[20] Adam and Eve were utterly open with each other, holding nothing back. They were fully transparent—delighting in the experience of knowing and being known in a perfect and secure love relationship. This is what God intends for us by creating us as relational beings in his image.

The Trinity: The Eternal Love Dance

Adam and Eve's one-flesh intimacy is strikingly beautiful, yet it reflects a much greater eternal intimacy. The Father, Son, and Spirit are three persons, yet they are completely, utterly, perfectly, and eternally united in their being, work, love, and purpose. This understanding of the Trinity

18. Smedes, *Sex for Christians*, 32–33.

19. "Nakedness" in the Hebrew Scriptures is most often used to refer to the humiliation of the poor (Job 24:7; Ezek 18:16) and refers to a sign of shame or guilt (Hos 2:3).

20. The Hebrew verb used here for shame (yitbōšāšû) is in the Hithpael stem and in the imperfect tense. Victor Hamilton argues that the force of the imperfect tense here is ongoing action, and the Hithpael stem here denotes reciprocity. *The Book of Genesis*, 181.

lays an essential foundation for understanding, delighting in, and worshipping the God of Scripture: Father, Son, and Spirit. Finding our delight and soul satisfaction in God, developing intimacy with him, *is* the foundation for all other intimacies. Only then will we have the ability to develop the same kind of oneness in our relationships evidenced in God's reciprocal love within himself.[21] In a sense, we are swept up into that reciprocal love of the Father, Son, and Spirit.

The love and delight the Father, Son, and Spirit have for and with each other is clearly revealed in the New Testament. For instance, immediately after Jesus was baptized by John, "suddenly the heavens were opened to him and he saw the Spirit of God descending like a dove and alighting on him. And a voice from heaven said, 'This is my Son, the Beloved, with whom I am well pleased.'"[22] Thus, at the outset of Jesus' public ministry, we have a powerful picture of the Father and the Spirit delighting in the Son. Furthermore, John tells us the Father and Son know each other, love each other, and are one with each other (John 10:15–18, 30). The unity and intimacy of the Trinity is more than the most intense and mature love between two human beings because the three members of the Trinity share not just love, but the divine life itself. John 14:10–11 states:

> Do you not believe that I am in the Father and the Father is in me? The words that I say to you I do not speak on my own; but the Father who dwells in me does his works. Believe me that I am in the Father and the Father is in me; but if you do not, then believe me because of the works themselves. (NRSV)

Thus, there is a very rich, ancient history in Christian theology of understanding God's being as a "communion." Relationship and intimacy lie at the heart of his existence.[23] In fact, God is so fundamentally relational that "without the concept of communion it would not be possible to speak of the Being of God."[24] One of the greatest modern experts on the doctrine of the Trinity states that God is anything but impersonal,

---

21. John 14:9–10; 10:30; 17:5.

22. Matt 3:16–17; cp. Matt 12:17–21; 17:5.

23. The fourth-century church father Basil seems to be the first to articulate this concept, for he used the Greek word *koinonia* to describe how Father, Son, and Spirit are inseparably united and coactive in all of their actions and are of one essential nature, *De Spiritu Sancto*, 37, 45.

24. Ziziouslas, *Being as Communion*, 17.

for "he is a Communion of personal Being within himself, for the whole God dwells in each person, and each Person is the whole God. Thus we may rightly think . . . of the Triune God as intrinsically, perfectly, and sublimely personal."[25] The church fathers brilliantly described the mystery, beauty, and richness of the way God eternally exists as one divine being in three distinct persons through the doctrine of *perichoresis*. This term comes from a compound word in Greek and refers to the "mutual indwelling," or better, "mutual interpenetration" of the Triune God.[26] It has been described as an eternal and dynamic "circle of reciprocal relations."[27] This is not a static concept, but a very dynamic reality in our lives and relationships. We essentially are swept up into the eternal movement of the love of the Father, the Son, and the Holy Spirit for one another, which flows outward unceasingly toward us. This truth of God's intimacy within himself flowing beyond himself to believers who in turn allow his love to flow to unbelievers is seen in John 17:21–23:

> [T]hat all of them may be one,
> Father, just as you are in me and I am in you.
> May they also be in us so that the world may believe that you have sent me.
> I have given them the glory that you gave me,
> that they may be one as we are one:
> I in them and you in me.
> May they be brought to complete unity
> to let the world know that you sent me
> and have loved them even as you have loved me. (NIV)

The essential point here is that intimacy comes from God. He is the ultimate source of love. Thus, love is a defining characteristic of his children. John states this succinctly: "Beloved, let us love one another, because love is from God; everyone who loves is born of God and knows God" (1 John 4:7). The New Testament links God's love to human love in various ways. The Father's relationship with the Son is given as the paradigm for male/female relationships (1 Cor 11:3). Christ's love for the church is the paradigm for husbands' sacrificial care of their wives

25. Torrance, *The Christian Doctrine of God*, 202.

26. Smith, "Perichoresis." The theological term *perichoresis* is an English transliteration of the Greek term, which is composed of two words/word groups and indicates a "co-indwelling."

27. Torrance, *The Christian Doctrine of God*, 174.

(Eph 5:25–30). More specifically applied, just as the husband physically penetrates his wife in sexual expressions of love, so are his emotional and relational initiations of love to "penetrate" his wife and mirror Christ's initiations of love to us, his bride. The believers' experience of intimacy with Christ and the Holy Spirit leads to unity and loving care among believers (Phil 2:1–4). Hence, the more we grow in our intimacy with God, the more we will reflect his character by extending his love to others.

The power of the *sweep* of God's love, flowing out of his own being to us and then through us to others, is breathtaking, particularly when it extends to those shattered by hurtful and evil human relationships. Our youngest daughter, Abby, lives in Kampala, Uganda, and ministers to street children in one of the country's poorest slums. Virtually all of her children have experienced chronic physical, verbal, and often sexual abuse. They live like animals and are treated worse than animals. Abby often describes her ministry as being "God in skin" to the most marginalized and destitute. She initially had no idea how damaged "the least of these" are in African slums. Hence, she could not imagine how thoroughly the sweep of God's love could work miracles. In her online blog, Abby recounts her first day of ministry to these children of the streets:

> That first day I was shocked to see how terrible the lives of the street kids were. I had known that they were difficult. I had worked with many former street children. I had written numerous research papers about them. I had spent a lot of time in slum areas of developing countries. And yet, even after all of that, I was not prepared for my first day on the streets working with these kids. I came with a heart that God had already given me, that was overflowing with love for those kids, and somehow each second that I spent with them continued to increase that love more and more.
>
> Barely clothed, in filthy and tattered garments, most of the children were shoeless, digging in garbage dumps where they were living. They were covered in dirt and grime that over time had accumulated into an aroma that was distinct and overpowering. Many were suffering from festering wounds. All of those precious kids, young and old, were constantly using drugs, and I mean constantly. Most of them were inhaling a petrol-like substance from bottles and rags that dulled their senses—killing their brain cells while at the same time subduing their feelings of hunger, neglect, trauma, and physical pain. I was surprised that first day by the fierceness of these children. I had expected a few

wide-eyed and hungry kids who just needed a hug and a warm meal. What I found was an endless stream of angry and abused children who did not trust anyone, were hungry, thirsty, tired, beaten down, hopeless, wanting to fight, drugged, and sad. It was such a bigger problem than I had ever realized. That day ignited in me a passion not only to understand these street kids, but to work my way slowly but surely into their lives and hearts.[28]

Abby and her ministry colleagues eventually built a home in the village of Ssengi and took some of the youngest boys into it to live with them. They continued daily to visit the children still in the slums, caring for them physically, emotionally, and spiritually. Abby did work her way into these hardened children's hearts. They, and Abby, were transformed by the love of God. She described the miraculous, life-changing power of the sweep of God's love as follows:

The children we have taken off the streets into the Ssengi home are not the same children I first met. They began to demonstrate what amazing boys they really were, once they knew they were loved. They wanted me to call them "my child," rather than by their first name. They would rush to help me when they thought I needed it, show me the school work that they had completed, and tell me about their day. The boys still on the streets share every bit of food they have with me and make sure that they take care of me. They always hold my hand when we walk through the slums so that I won't slip in the grime, clean it off for me if I do, and fight to sit next to me so that they can have their back rubbed, falling asleep in my lap. They are not the same boys; God is completely transforming their lives. There have been times as I walk downtown, when a group of wild street kids, tugging at any piece of my arm or hand that they can touch, that I thank God for my life. I love my life. Looking at some of those boys and simply thinking of how amazing they were, brought tears to my eyes—I loved them so much. It brings tears to my eyes just typing this that for some reason, God chose me to be hope to these precious street children. He chose me to take them into my arms and be His hands and feet as I show them what it is like to be loved and tell them about a Heavenly Father that loves them so much.

28. Abby Tracy's Live Journal is at: http://africa-love.livejournal.com.

The Sweep of Scripture: The Power and Promise of Intimacy

Abby's specific circumstances and experience of the powerful sweep of God's love are unusual. As she puts it, "Few people are as blessed as I am to be able to work with street children." However, experiencing life-transforming intimacy should be normative for all believers, for intimacy with God and with other believers summarizes salvation—past, present, and future.

SALVATION: NEW INTIMACY WITH GOD AND BELIEVERS

Salvation is a beautifully rich doctrine involving many different, overlapping doctrines and divine actions. It encompasses some of the most intricate theological debates. Yet, at the heart of this multifaceted doctrine lie two foundational truths: (1) The greatest tragedy in human history is that sin has alienated us from God our Creator. Our supreme human need is relational. (2) The greatest triumph in human history took place on the cross, for "in Christ God was reconciling the world to himself" (2 Cor 5:19). God so values intimacy with us that he was willing to pay the greatest imaginable price to meet our greatest imaginable need. God did this in spite of the fact that we cannot give him anything he is lacking. He has enjoyed perfect intimacy in his own Divine Being from eternity past. Such is the incomprehensible beauty of God's love—He delights in intimacy with alienated, sinful human beings. C. S. Lewis captures well the mystery of God's love, which places the highest value on intimacy with fallen humans:

> God, who needs nothing, loves into existence wholly superfluous creatures in order that He may love and perfect them. He creates the universe, already foreseeing . . . the buzzing cloud of flies above the cross, the flayed back pressed against the uneven stake, the nails driven through the mesial nerves, the repeated incipient suffocation as the body droops, the repeated torture of back and arms, as it is time after time, for breath's sake hitched up. If I may dare the biological image, God is a "host" who deliberately creates his own parasites; causes us to be that we might exploit and "take advantage" of Him. Herein is love. This is the diagram of Love Himself, the inventor of all loves.[29]

The human experience of the love of God in salvation brings a breathtaking level of intimacy with God and with other believers.

29. Lewis, *The Four Loves*, 176.

Believers become God's friends, brothers and sisters of Christ, joint heirs with Christ, and beloved sons and daughters of God.[30] Believers are described as being united with Christ so intimately that his life becomes their life. Thus, Paul says that, when Christ died, we died; when Christ was raised from the dead, we were raised to new life (Rom 6:3–11). Believers' intimacy with God is so complete that they are indwelled by God himself (John 14:16–20). Furthermore, salvation brings one into a new community, creating a new living "body" to which all believers belong (1 Cor 12:12–26). Our oneness with other believers is so profound that, if one fellow believer suffers or is honored, it is as if all believers experience this (1 Cor 12:26). This oneness is so powerful that it reconciles alienated people groups and eradicates all divisive ethnic and gender identities (Eph 2:14–16, Gal 3:28). Unity among believers is one of the surest evidences of the truthfulness of the gospel (John 17:20–23). In fact, loving intimacy among believers is so valuable that it is better to allow a fellow believer to cheat you financially than to sue him or her in court and shout to the world that the Christian community is no different than the rest of the estranged world, since Christians cannot work out their differences (1 Cor 6:1–8).

SANCTIFICATION: DEEPENED INTIMACY WITH GOD THROUGH RELATIONSHIPS

Sanctification centers on deepening one's intimacy with God. This happens through the believers' relationships with the Holy Spirit and other believers. The key word here is *growing* intimacy with God. Based on the teachings of Scripture, we affirm the wonderful intimacy with God that salvation brings. Yet, in this life, our experience rarely, if ever, seems to match the intimacy we are said to possess. While we have been united and raised with Christ and are called saints, we inhabit this world, not heaven. We struggle to experience God's presence, let alone union with him. The problem is not on God's side of the relationship—he has reconciled himself to believers and declares us his beloved children. The challenge is that salvation is a process that culminates in glorification when believers will be perfected in intimacy with God. Until then, believers are in the process of being sanctified—that is, becoming increasingly intimate with Christ by becoming more like him.[31] Our longings for

30. John 15:15; Rom 8:17, 29; Heb 12:6–8.
31. Rom 8:29; 1 Cor 15:49; 2 Cor 3:18.

more intimacy with God beckon us forward. Our hope for the intimacy we will someday experience should give us strength and motivation to grow in the present. The Apostle John states this well: "Beloved, we are God's children now; what we will be has not yet been revealed. What we do know is this: when he is revealed, we will be like him, for we will see him as he is. And all who have this hope in him purify themselves as he is pure" (1 John 3:2–3). C. S. Lewis similarly describes the battle to experience more intimacy with God in terms of the "shape of the gap where our love of God ought to be." This frustrating gap evidences the fact that we are made for deeper intimacy with God and will someday experience it. This should drive us toward God in this life. Lewis says that, while this gap in our love for God

> is not enough. It is something. If we cannot "practice the presence of God," it is something to practice the absence of God, to become increasingly aware of our unawareness till we feel like men who should stand beside a great cataract and hear no noise, or like a man in a story who looks in a mirror and finds no face there, or a man in a dream who stretches out his hand to visible objects and gets no sensation of touch. To know one is dreaming is to be no longer perfectly asleep.[32]

Believers are no longer perfectly asleep—they have begun to taste intimacy with God and long for more. Thankfully, sanctification is characterized by growing intimacy with God. How does this take place? We often long for foolproof, impersonal formulas for spiritual growth. This is the appeal of legalism—do this, don't do that, and you will be spiritual. Furthermore, everyone else will know whether or not you are spiritual simply by looking at whether or not you keep the rules. Scripture, however, teaches that sanctification takes place not through rigid rule keeping (the law), but through intimate relationship.[33] The Apostle Paul, in particular, emphasizes that the process of spiritual growth is an intensely relational one, empowered by the Holy Spirit who indwells all believers. More specifically, sanctification happens as believers live by the Spirit,

---

32. Lewis, *The Four Loves*, 192.

33. This is particularly seen in Galatians, where Paul refutes the power of the law to sanctify, instead emphasizing life in the Spirit. For an academic development of this issue in Galatians, see Barclay, *Obeying the Truth*.

are guided by the Spirit, yield to the Spirit, and do not grieve or quench the Spirit.[34]

Another layer of intimacy is involved in sanctification. We do not build an intimate relationship with God through the Spirit on our own. Sanctification happens in human community through intimate relationship with other believers. This process is reflected, for example, in the many "one another" commands in the New Testament. Just a few of these deeply relational commands follow. Many of them are explicitly grounded in the love believers experience with God:

> Love one another with mutual affection; outdo one another in showing honor. (Rom 12:10)

> Welcome one another, therefore, just as Christ has welcomed you, for the glory of God. (Rom 15:7)

> Bear one another's burdens, and in this way you will fulfill the law of Christ. (Gal 6:2)

> [B]e kind to one another, tenderhearted, forgiving one another, as God in Christ has forgiven you. (Eph 4:32)

> Bear with one another and, if anyone has a complaint against another, forgive each other; just as the Lord has forgiven you, so you also must forgive. (Col 3:13)

> Let the word of Christ dwell in you richly; teach and admonish one another in all wisdom. (Col 3:16)

> And let us consider how to provoke one another to love and good deeds, not neglecting to meet together, as is the habit of some, but encouraging one another. (Heb 10:24–25)

> Therefore confess your sins to one another, and pray for one another, so that you may be healed. (Jas 5:16)

In summary, sanctification, from start to finish, is relational. It involves becoming more intimate with God by becoming more like Christ. This happens not through obeying impersonal rules, but through pursuing intimate relationship with the Spirit. Furthermore, sanctification takes place in community with other believers. We cannot become more intimate with God apart from intimacy with other believers.

---

34. Gal 5:16, 25; Eph 4:30; 1 Thess 5:19.

ETERNITY: UTTER INTIMACY WITH ETERNAL GOD

The story of Scripture is the restoration of intimacy. Adam and Eve's sin caused them to be separated from God, alienated from each other, and removed from God's presence in the garden of Eden. One day, all believers will enjoy perfect intimacy with God and with each other for all eternity. The biblical descriptions of heaven are thus magnificently relational and intimate. Though now we only enjoy a glimpse of God, as if seeing him dimly through hazy glass, the day is coming when we will see God "face to face." Though we have only partial knowledge now, the day is coming when we "will know fully" even as we "have been fully known" (1 Cor 13:12–13). Revelation 7:9–17 gives a majestic picture of heaven as a place of perfect community where people of every nation, tribe, and tongue are united, along with the holy angels, in worshipping Christ. Their unity is driven by their common intimacy with Christ the Lamb who "will be their shepherd." Later in Revelation, when God creates a new heaven and a new earth, it is described as a place of complete intimacy with God: "See, the home of God is among mortals. He will dwell with them and they will be his peoples, and God himself will be with them" (Rev 21:3). We can only long for and imagine the joy and oneness we will experience with God in heaven, but our closest glimpse may well be the joy and closeness a husband and wife experience when they celebrate their love in sexual intimacy. Scripture may hint at this by describing a wedding feast in heaven for believers who are the bride of Christ (Rev 19:7–9).[35]

Hell, on the other hand, is the opposite of heaven. Hell is repeatedly described in terms of isolation, aloneness, darkness. In the final judgment, unbelievers are described as being cast out or shut out of God's presence, separated from God's presence, shut out of the marriage feast, banished into outer darkness, and banished from the New Jerusalem.[36] The separation from God that unbelievers experience does not annul

35. Thus, the question "will there be sex in heaven?" is not as irrelevant or irreverent as it might seem. In fact, Peter Kreeft argues "Even the most satisfying earthly intercourse between spouses cannot perfectly express all their love. If the possibility of intercourse in heaven is not actualized, it is only for the same reason earthly lovers do not eat candy during intercourse: there is something much better to do." He concludes by saying "this spiritual intercourse with God is the ecstasy hinted at in all earthly intercourse, physical or spiritual. (Kreeft, "Is There Sex in Heaven?") See also P. Shepherd, "Sex in Heaven?"

36. Matt 7:23; 25:41; 2 Thess 1:9; Matt 25:10–12; Matt 8:12; Rev 22:15.

God's loving desire for intimacy with humans, but actually flows out of it. Hence, Stanley Grenz describes hell as the "dark side of God's love."

> God is an eternal lover. In keeping with his own nature, he loves his creation eternally, and he desires that humans respond to his love by enjoying unending fellowship with him. We dare not confuse God's love with his sentimentality. As the great Lover, God is also the avenging protector of the love relationship. Consequently, God's love has a dark side. Those who spurn or seek to destroy the holy love relationship God desires to enjoy with creation experience the divine love as protective jealousy or wrath.[37]

From inception to consummation, human salvation and judgment revolve around God's commitment to establish an intimate love relationship with humans. We were made for intimacy because we are made in the image of the perfectly intimate God. It is our design. For believers, it is our destiny.

CONCLUSION

A young man once came to see me (Celestia) for counseling. Though he was bright and accomplished, he was deeply discouraged and desperate for help. During our first few sessions, Bill recounted a twenty-year history of shallow, strained, and failed relationships. He was lonely and keenly longed to be married, yet felt that he lacked the most rudimentary relational skills. Worse yet, he likened himself to "Edward Scissorhands," the fictional movie character who, despite his best intentions, manages to damage everything he touches, for he was born with blades instead of hands. Many of us can relate to Bill's frustration. We deeply, innately long for intimacy; we are wired for it from birth; it is essential to our wellbeing. Yet, as we look at human history and our personal history, it feels as if we have relational "scissor hands" and are wired to sabotage intimacy instead. We will address this in the following chapter—"Intimacy Disrupted."

---

37. Grenz, *Theology for the Community of God*, 836.

2

Intimacy Disrupted

> Do you want me to tell you something subversive? Love is everything it's cracked up to be. That's why people are so cynical about it. It really is worth fighting for, being brave for, risking everything for. And the trouble is, if you don't risk anything, you risk even more.
>
> —Erica Jong

ERICA JONG EVIDENCES PROFOUND insight into human intimacy in this short quotation. Love *is* all it's cracked up to be. Love *is* worth fighting for. And yet, because failed relationships can generate overflowing rivers of cynicism, we must continue to take the risk of loving. Ironically, Jong's own life evidences the challenge of experiencing intimacy in a broken world. Jong, an influential and successful author, is known particularly for her promotion of casual sex. She unabashedly chronicles her own sexual escapades, including numerous casual sexual relationships and several marital affairs, including one with Martha Stewart's former husband, Andy Stewart. Martha reportedly blames Erica for the breakup of her marriage.[1] Jong is on her fourth marriage, which has lasted almost twenty years. Jong's daughter Molly, also an author, has written of her painful childhood and what would appear to be the damaging effects of her mother's sexual libertinism.[2] In one of her most recent works, Erica acknowledges regret over some of her past sexual choices and resultant relational consequences. In commenting on her affair with Andy Stewart, she describes seeing Martha on television or in print and thinking, "Does she trust anyone? It's hard to trust, and I didn't make it any

1. Jong, "Scenes from an Open Marriage."
2. Jong-Fast, *Girl [Maladjusted]*.

easier for her. When you can't trust anyone, there's no choice but to wind up alone. A blasted marriage can also blast your heart."[3]

Despite our best efforts, intimate relationships are incredibly difficult to cultivate. Most of us have had our heart "blasted" by someone we cared for deeply and trusted. Just when we think we have found real love, we, our friend or partner, or a third party sabotages the relationship. After a while, many simply give up on the intimacy their hearts crave. Sadly, it appears that in twenty-first-century America, intimate relationships are an increasingly endangered species. For instance, between 1985 and 2004, the number of confidants—close friends people shared "important matters" with—dropped by one-third (from three people to two). Worse yet, the number of people who said they had no one with whom they shared important matters tripled between 1985 and 2004. Roughly one-quarter of those surveyed in 2004 shared important matters with no one.[4] Thus, it is not surprising to find that, based on the 2000 U.S. census, there are more Americans living alone than at any time in U.S. history (one-forth of all households).[5] The situation is even worse in Europe, particularly among younger adults.[6] Since all humans are wired for intimacy, why is it so elusive?

SATAN'S STRATEGY

The ubiquitous human struggle for intimacy is no accident. We no longer live in Eden; we now contend with internal and external forces that imperil any and every relationship. Given the fact that being made in God's image means we have a deep capacity, longing, and need for intimacy, and given the fact that human intimacy carries God-like power (the ability to create life), it should come as no surprise that *Satan's greatest goal is to disrupt human relationships.* He desires to shatter all of our most meaningful connections—with God, family, and others—and has crafted countless malevolent strategies for achieving this devious plan.

This is precisely what we see in the biblical account of the first human temptation and sin in Genesis 3:1–19. It is no accident that this description, with its hideous relational consequences, falls immediately

3. Erica Jong, "Scenes from an Open Marriage."

4. McPherson, Smith-Lovin, and Brashears, "Social Isolation in America." See also Putnam, *Bowling Alone.*

5. Olds and Schwartz, *The Lonely American,* 2.

6. Chandler et al., "Living Alone."

after the final paragraph of chapter 2, which summarizes the fulfillment of God's beautiful plan for human intimacy: "And they will become one flesh. The man and his wife were both naked, and they felt no shame." However, this Edenic oneness was about to be viciously shattered. The serpent, energized by Satan himself, began a crafty dialogue with Eve designed to make disobedience to God the most logical and appealing act imaginable. He does this with a threefold series of escalating questions and statements that created doubt about God's word ("Did God really say"), discredited God's word ("You will not surely die"), and maligned God's character ("God knows that when you eat of it your eyes will be opened, and you will be like God"). Once the seeds of distrust had been sown, disobedience was a foregone conclusion. So Eve and Adam ate the forbidden fruit and instantly, permanently altered the course of human history. From this moment on, every human being born would know the pain of loneliness and fractured intimacy.

God didn't need to tell Adam and Eve their intimacy with him had been shattered; they felt their alienation in the form of gut-wrenching shame and fear, immediately hiding from God and each other. Shame, the sense that something is terribly wrong within us, is one of the most powerful human experiences. Shame, in turn, creates inescapable fear that haunts and dogs us—fear of being discovered, fear of being rejected, fear of punishment, and fear of being exposed for what we really are: guilty, defective, and irredeemable. Hence, many of our waking moments are spent consciously and subconsciously hiding our true imperfect selves from those around us. We then create sanitized "press releases" of our personal lives and histories that protect us from exposure and rejection, yet also keep us from the deepest hunger of our soul—being truly known and loved.

For this reason, after his mother died, Frederick Buechner wrote a personal memoir entitled *Telling Secrets,* in which he lays bare the secrets of his own family, including his daughter's anorexia as well as the most fiercely guarded and influential family secret of all, his father's suicide.[7] Buechner later tells why he took the risk of baring his own ugly secrets to the English-speaking world,

> [W]hat we hunger for more than anything else is to be known in
> our full humanness, and yet that is often just what we also fear
> more than anything else. It is important to tell at least from time

7. Buechner, *Telling Secrets.*

to time the secret of who we truly and fully are—even if we tell it only to ourselves—because otherwise we run the risk of losing track of who we truly and fully are and little by little come to accept instead the highly edited version which we put forth in hope that the world will find it more acceptable than the real thing.[8]

In terms of human intimacy, it is monumentally significant that the first thing that happened to Adam and Eve when they sinned was that they became painfully aware of their nakedness. There were no other humans in existence to see their unclothed bodies, yet they were now embarrassed at having their genitals exposed to the spouse given to them by God. Hence, their first post-fall action was to make fig leaf loincloths. Unless you have picked figs recently, the obvious implication of this primordial wardrobe might be missed easily. Fig leaves are incredibly rough and have a sandpaper-like texture.[9] Imagine how irritating these "clothes" would have been. In their fear and shame, Adam and Eve were desperate to hide their most personal physical selves from each other. We, like them, are prone to take extreme measures to avoid the perceived risk of real exposure. Not only does our shame isolate us from each other, it isolates us from God (Gen 3:8).

Centuries later, Satan has not changed his master plan. He fixates on disrupting and sabotaging intimacy in two primary ways. First of all, Satan tempts us to meet legitimate needs in illegitimate ways. Eve had a legitimate need for food, and the fruit on the Tree of the Knowledge of Good and Evil was made by God, but this was not a valid way to satisfy her hunger. Satiating her appetite through disobedience resulted in unimaginable long-term hunger. Similarly, in 1 Corinthians 7:1–5, Paul instructs married couples to have sexual relations on a regular basis so that Satan will not tempt them to meet their legitimate sexual needs with someone other than their spouse. Again, Satan, seizing on normal, healthy needs, tempted Corinthian husbands and wives to meet those needs through sexual relations outside of marriage. This would destroy their marital intimacy (cf. Matt 19:9) as well as intimacy with their heavenly Father (cf. 1 Cor 6:9).

8. Buechner, *Listening to Your Life*, 318.

9. Victor P. Hamilton notes that the fig tree has the largest leaves of any tree in Palestine, and may have had some of the largest leaves of any trees in the garden of Eden. Thus, Adam and Eve likely chose fig leaves because they would have given the greatest amount of covering. *The Book of Genesis*, 191.

Satan's second strategy builds on the first. He offers the allure of real intimacy without the apparent cost. True intimacy involves vulnerability, risk taking, unselfish sacrifice, and relational surrender. Real intimacy is costly, though sidestepping intimacy is even more so. C. S. Lewis brilliantly articulates the cost of real intimacy and the subtle, yet real, price of avoiding this cost. He states:

> To love at all is to be vulnerable. Love anything, and your heart will certainly be wrung and possibly broken. If you want to make sure of keeping it intact, you must give your heart to no one, not even to an animal. Wrap it carefully round with hobbies and little luxuries; avoid all entanglements; lock it safe in the casket or coffin of your selfishness. But in that casket—safe, dark, motionless, airless—it will change. It will not be broken; it will become unbreakable, impenetrable, irredeemable. . . . The only place outside Heaven where you can be perfectly safe from all the dangers and perturbations of love is Hell.[10]

So, in light of the risks inherent in real love, Satan tempts us with shortcuts toward the experience of the delights of intimacy—sexual pleasure, affection, being appreciated, being loved, belonging, and validation. He deceives us into believing that we can have real intimacy without taking relational risks or paying the price for real love. The Hebrew Scriptures graphically illustrate this temptation with two distinct phrases used to describe sexual relations. In marriage, sexual intercourse is beautifully described with the Hebrew verb *yadah,* which means "to know." This is what Adam did with Eve in Genesis 4:1, resulting in the conception of their son Cain. This language for marital sexual intimacy depicts a deep soul connection celebrated through sexual union. Knowing a spouse in this fuller, deeper sense takes time, patience, and much hard work. Notice that this is not what David did with Bathsheba—he lay with her (2 Sam 11:4). David experienced the sexual pleasure and the allure of intimacy, but it was a destructive counterfeit. It was merely copulating with someone's genitals, not knowing and connecting with one's soul.

Several years ago in a counseling session, I (Steve) witnessed the stark contrast between genuine and counterfeit intimacy in an unforgettable conversation. George had come to see me because his wife had moved out and was threatening to divorce him unless he immediately

10. Lewis, *The Four Loves,* 169.

initiated intensive counseling.[11] She gave this ultimatum after receiving a call from the manager of a local hotel who reported that her husband had just rented a room with a prostitute. While I applauded this owner's unflinching honesty, I was intrigued that he would boldly jeopardize his client base in this way. This was certainly not an effective marketing plan! When I met with George, I asked him what prompted the owner to call his wife. Apparently, shortly before George's infamous liaison, the hotel owner's wife of more than thirty years had died after a protracted battle with cancer. This husband lovingly cared for her until the end. He was devastated that the love of his life had been taken from him. So, when George waltzed in with a prostitute in tow, in spite of the fact that he had a wedding ring on his finger, the hotel owner simply could not allow such a travesty to go unchallenged. Thankfully, George eventually saw his actions for what they were—a gross perversion of intimacy. In fact, after he was caught, the single factor that most troubled George was that he had no recollection whatsoever of the prostitute's face. He realized that, in bleak contrast to the hotel owner, he hadn't experienced the slightest shred of relational connection, let alone intimacy, in his promiscuous affairs. George's counterfeit intimacy was proving hollow, unsatisfying, and extremely costly.

Satan has far more weapons in his intimacy-wrecking arsenal, however, than sex. He uses our own relational laziness and fear of others' pain to keep us stuck in shallow and unsatisfying relationships. In our pleasure-driven culture, we are constantly tempted to play relational games to avoid the work, discomfort, and disruption that intimacy requires. Shallowness has become a cultural norm.

Recently, after a day's research on the contrast between real and false intimacy, I went on a magnificent forest hike. At the trailhead, I met a family on their way back down the mountain. As we drew closer to each other, the father shot me a quick glance and queried, "How are you?" I answered with the customary social response, "Great!" to which he immediately replied, "Wonderful." Since I love few activities more than hiking the San Juan Mountains, my answer to his greeting was not dishonest. However, I wondered how he would have responded had I given a more complete answer. I could have said, "Actually my wife is

---

11. For several years, I conducted individual pastoral counseling and led groups for men struggling with sexual compulsion.

having some serious medical tests in a few days. She has a degenerative disease, and I am quite concerned about her."

Often, we do not really want to know the deeper painful realities that lurk beneath our polished surfaces. It is "Great!" if others do not break the illusion that all is well. Christians are certainly not immune from this common intimacy-buster of shallow and safe conversations, maintaining illusions that everything is just fine. In fact, I find that often we Christians can be more dishonest and superficial than unbelievers. For instance, when working with male sex addicts, I learned the hard way that many Christian accountability groups were shallower, and, hence, less effective than similar secular support groups. In Alcoholics Anonymous or Sexaholics Anonymous, if someone has had a really bad week, they are often more likely to admit this and participants are more likely to demand honesty if they don't.

As Christians, we often believe we shouldn't struggle with sin, doubt, or discouragement, so we simply pretend we don't. Thus, we shy away from entering into others' pain and, instead, perpetuate the pretense that all is well. Our pretense, however, undercuts intimacy and keeps us from being truly known, embraced, and loved. It keeps us from being what God calls us to be—a truly intimate community that is honest, real, and tenaciously pursuing each other in love. We see this type of Christian intimacy reflected in many New Testament commands directed at our relationships with fellow believers: "Rejoice with those who rejoice; mourn with those who mourn" (Rom 12:15); "Carry each another's burdens" (Gal 6:2); "Confess your sins to each other and pray for each other" (Jas 5:16); "Warn those who are idle, encourage the timid, help the weak, be patient with everyone" (1 Thess 5:14).

DANGEROUS CULTURAL SHIFTS

While Satan's strategy to disrupt intimacy remains constant through-out human history, each generation faces its own specific challenges to healthy relationships. For twenty-five years, we have offered academic, pastoral, and counseling support to singles and couples, helping them repair and build healthy relationships. Over these years of ministry, we have observed several cultural shifts that are dramatically impacting our relationships.

Shift #1: The Power of the Internet

The Internet is arguably the most significant technological advancement since Christ walked the earth. It has completely transformed the nature of business, education, recreation, and relationships. Most of us are so comfortable interacting with friends and associates online that we are unaware of the ways in which the Internet compromises true intimacy. The deception of our technological explosion is that, at first blush, it appears to have enhanced relationships. With the availability of instant information about others combined with the ability to communicate instantly from virtually anywhere in the world, the Internet would appear to enhance our relationships. Web sites such as Facebook and MySpace give unprecedented opportunities for social networking, allowing people to tell their friends and the world about themselves. Many post online journals giving their friends access to their most personal thoughts and photos. However, the relational potential of the Internet is not all it appears to be.

First of all, the Internet gives us a heightened but false sense of relational control. Online, we can reveal only as much of ourselves as we choose. We can communicate for months or even years with someone who never really knows us. We can easily give deceptive information, including pictures of ourselves that are completely fabricated. For instance, Dateline NBC broadcasts a series of extremely popular programs hosted by Chris Hanson entitled "To Catch a Predator." These shows consist of hidden camera recordings of alleged sexual predators coming to a prearranged location to have sexual relations with adolescent girls. These men allegedly think they have been interacting online with naïve adolescent girls whom they intend to exploit. However, in reality, they have been interacting with streetwise, middle-aged investigators who will happily assist with their criminal prosecution. While this is the extreme end of Internet relational dysfunction, there are countless smaller ways in which the Internet allows us to maintain control by editing our true selves as we "relate" to others.

In a real conversation, we cannot delete someone simply because they annoy us! However, we can choose to answer our emails when or if we want to, answer our phones when or if we want to, disclose what we want, when we want, and in whatever way we want. As one young adult narcissistically described a former roommate who offended her, "Now that I have taken her off of my buddy list, she no longer exists." In clear contrast, real intimacy requires time and energy for disclosure, honesty, and respectful conflict resolution—all of which are easily avoided on the Internet.

The Internet also retards intimacy by limiting communication to mere words. Psychologists have found that 93 percent of human communication is nonverbal. In other words, the vast majority of what we communicate to others comes not through our words themselves, but through inflection, facial gestures, tone of voice, eye contact, and body language.[12] And virtually none of these nonverbal messages is communicated through email. Additionally, when we have just words and no visual image of the person we are communicating with, we can easily create fantasies about him or her. It is much easier to manipulate another person in our mind, making them who we want them to be, when we have never seen or heard that person. Intimacy is predicated on reality, not a fabricated and false fantasy.

With the technological glut of instant information and sophisticated services online, we can deceive ourselves into thinking that we can simply "find" intimacy. In other words, the Internet feeds the myth that we can find our soul mate with a quick click of the mouse rather than carefully creating a love-of-a-lifetime through sacrifice, risk, and commitment. A plethora of social networking sites feeds this pervasive relational myth. For instance, one popular Internet dating service not only lets you select specific physical characteristics, such as body type and shape of lips, nose, and breasts, but also personality and "compatibility" characteristics. Another site promises to find you the perfect "match of your dreams."

As a part of our research for this book I (Celestia) went to a popular online dating service Web site and filled out the personality profile within the application. I was given both a printout of my personality and the type of corresponding personality profiles I needed for a "perfect match." Within hours, I was informed that *two* compatible matches had been discovered in my community. I have to say that this was not an encouraging finding, as we live in one of the largest cities in the U.S.! For a nominal fee, I could have the contact information for these two

---

12. Research shows that 55 percent of communication comes from nonverbal body language and gestures, 38 percent comes from voice (pitch, speed, intensity, etc.) and only 7 percent comes from the bare words. See Mehrabian and Ferris, "Inference of Attitudes from Nonverbal Communication."

men. I was told that the "compatible" characteristics I would need in a partner were playful, fast-acting, and a frequent use of humor. What is most interesting to me in reading my profile, and the profiles of my two "matches," is that I am squarely in the middle of a deeply satisfying and stimulating relationship with my life partner of more than thirty years. Steve is none of the things my profile said he needed to be. In fact, his methodical and stabilizing temperament has been most beneficial and complementary in our relationship. I am more heart—passionate, emotional, and sometimes impulsive. He is more head—cautious, intellectual, and consistently stable. These individual differences have required a great deal of unselfishness, work, and time to create the attachment we enjoy today. God has used the crucible of our marriage to produce his best fruit in us. Today, my husband and I share a life and work that we passionately love. It took a dogged determination and covenant commitment to learn to love each other well. For us, the sum has turned out to be much greater than the parts. My soul mate was not found, but created; over time we were molded into the shape of the other's soul.

Shift #2: Pornography

It would be difficult, if not impossible, for us to overestimate the impact of pornography on contemporary relationships. It is radically altering and transforming our society. While pornography has existed for thousands of years, today's pornography is dramatically different. It is much more graphic, accessible, and socially acceptable than ever before.[13] In 2004, ComScore, an Internet tracking company, found that more than 70 percent of men ages eighteen to thirty-four visit one or more pornographic Web sites in a typical month.[14] Legal pornography is now estimated to be a $12 billion industry in America.[15] To put this figure in perspective, it is more than the combined revenues of ABC, CBS, and NBC, and more than the revenue of all professional baseball, football, and basketball teams put together. With such massive profits, it is not surprising that pornography has entered mainstream America, both on Wall Street and in the neighborhood shopping mall. What used to be a

13. Barron and Kimmel, "Sexual Violence in Three Pornographic Media"; Robert Jensen, "Cruel to be Hard: Men and Pornography"; Sarracino and Scott, *The Porning of America*.

14. Turpin, "Not tonight darling, I'm online."

15. Ropelato, "Internet Pornography Statistics."

"dirty" and secret occupation is now cause for notoriety. For instance, Jenna Jamison, a pornography star with immediate name recognition by millions of Americans, wrote a bestselling autobiography in 2004 entitled *How to Make Love Like a Porn Star*. It was an instant success and was on the *New York Times* bestseller list for six weeks.

Pornography has an overwhelming, direct impact on those who consume it, as well as on their partners. It also has a broader, more insidious influence on all of us because our entire culture has become, as one secular writer describes it, "pornified."[16] Even if we don't personally view pornography, because it is so prolific, socially acceptable, and powerful, it directly or indirectly impacts how our wives and daughters are treated, how women view themselves, how we understand masculinity and femininity, and how Americans view sex and carry out their relationships. For the younger generation born into a pornified culture, pornography is their sex education.[17]

Sadly, Christian men and women appear to be viewing pornography at very high rates. According to a *Christianity Today* survey published in 2001, 33 percent of clergy and 36 percent of laity admitted visiting porn sites.[18] A 2003 survey by *Today's Christian Woman* found that 34 percent of their female readers admitted to intentionally accessing Internet porn.[19]

We believe pornography is the most destructive weapon Satan is using in our generation to destroy relational intimacy. Consider the following:

1. IN THE MOST VICIOUS MANNER IMAGINABLE, PORNOGRAPHY PERVERTS SEX, ONE OF GOD'S MOST PRECIOUS GIFTS.

God created sex to be the joyful, most intimate expression of love between two people who have made a lifelong covenant commitment to each other. Thus, marital sex is to be a beautiful picture of steadfast, unconditional love. I (Steve) am blessed to have heard my father say many times, "You were conceived in love. Your mother and I prayed that God would bless us with children. You and your brothers are the result of our love for each other." I watched my parents live out steadfast, tender

16. Paul, *Pornified*.
17. See Meyer, *Search for Intimacy*, 14.
18. Gardner, "Tangled in the Worst of the Web."
19. Richards, "Dirty Little Secret."

love for each other for more than fifty years of marriage and through many trials, including my mother's battle with breast cancer and my father's heart disease and stroke. What an incalculable contrast this portrait of sex is to the one offered in pornography. Pornography depicts sex as an animalistic act, devoid of commitment, let alone tender love. Pornography is solely about crass, instant self-gratification. Women are objectified and become simply body parts whose value lies merely in helping men ejaculate. Pornography programs the user's heart, mind, and body to take, not give; to lust, not love; to objectify, not know.

2. PORNOGRAPHY SLASHES THE JUGULAR VEIN OF INTIMACY BY UTTERLY DIVORCING SEX FROM RELATIONSHIP.

The pornography industry is predicated on this perverse fact. Those who use pornography have no relationship with the nude women they lust after—that is the point. They can create a pseudo-relationship with them that exists only in their fantasy world, a relationship in which they are entirely in control, are never rejected, satisfy their most selfish whims, and are never expected to give anything in return. They do not even need to know the woman's name. The nature of pornography itself reinforces the separation of sex from relationship. One of the bleakest evidences of this comes from researcher Diana Russell who, more than a decade ago, analyzed four "mainstream" pornography magazines and found that less than 5 percent of the sex acts depicted were "traditional" vaginal intercourse between a man and a woman.[20] She discovered that the vast bulk of even the milder types of pornography involve anal sex, bestiality, group sex, bondage, torture, and simulated rape.

3. PORNOGRAPHY PROGRAMS MEN TO DOMINATE, MISUSE, AND DISDAIN WOMEN AND PROGRAMS WOMEN TO ACCEPT SUCH TREATMENT.

Modern pornography is predicated on the misuse and abasement of women. In fact, this is the primary conclusion of Russell's careful analysis of pornography—it is inherently misogynistic.[21] We need not recount the sordid specifics other than to note that pornography has become dramatically more extreme and violent in the past decade, with increasingly common depictions of the brutalization of women.

20. Russell, *Dangerous Relationships*, 18.
21. Ibid., 26, 37–40. See also Jensen, Dines, and Russo, *Pornography*, 98–100.

Journalist Robert Jensen has carefully analyzed pornography and the pornography industry for years and argues that the cruelty of pornography is destroying men, women, and our collective culture. He laments this painful reality:

> It hurts to know that no matter who you are as a woman, you can be reduced to a thing to be penetrated, and that men will buy movies about that, and that in many of those movies your humiliation will be the central theme. It hurts to know that so much of the pornography that men are buying fuses sexual desire with cruelty. It hurts women, and men like it, and it hurts just to know that.[22]

IMPACT OF PORNOGRAPHY ON HUSBANDS/BOYFRIENDS [23]

In terms of intimacy, the following are some of the most common specific effects of pornography on the millions of men who use it:

1. MEN BECOME EMOTIONALLY DETACHED AND SHUT DOWN.

Men who regularly use pornography literally alter their cognitive/emotional faculties. Their brains become conditioned, through the intricate neurological and hormonal processes of the human anatomy, to enter into a "fantasy world" of mental lust. Because pornography, like many other forms of satanic counterfeits, is subject to the law of diminishing returns, users typically have to view more extreme forms of pornography and enter the mental fantasy world more frequently to experience the same level of sexual excitement. They then become increasingly detached from the real world around them, including the very spouse they vowed to love "till death do us part." Thus, wives of these men often describe their husbands as continually "checked out" and disconnected. Additionally, men who use pornography become very self-absorbed and insensitive to others, making them even more emotionally detached from their family. Finally, all but the most hard-hearted Christian husband who uses pornography feels guilt and shame for his behavior, so he

---

22. Jensen, *Getting Off*, 14.

23. A helpful basic overview of the impact of pornography on men is given by Mark Laaser, *Healing the Wounds of Sexual Addiction*. For an academic analysis of pornography and its impact on men, see Zillmann, "Effects of Prolonged Consumption of Pornography," 127–57, and Jensen, Dines, and Russo, *Pornography*.

is drawn to shut down his emotions even further to drown out his inner guilty conscience.[24]

2. MEN BECOME DISRESPECTFUL, DISDAINFUL, AND DISMISSIVE OF WOMEN.

Pornography deadens, objectifies, and hardens the heart, all of which cause users to devalue women. The overtly misogynistic, degrading nature of modern pornography accentuates this dynamic, causing men increasingly and globally to disdain and disrespect women.

3. MEN BECOME INCREASINGLY DISSATISFIED WITH THEIR WIVES' PHYSICAL FEATURES AND SEXUAL PERFORMANCE.[25]

Since pornography programs men to objectify and sexualize women, and it is based on fantasy rather than reality, research shows that male users quickly and dramatically become dissatisfied with their real-life wives, no matter how loving or attractive they are. I (Steve) can illustrate these first three impacts of pornography on men by noting the way these effects can sometimes be felt, even by strangers. I have learned to trust Celestia's intuition when, after even a brief interaction with a man, she tells me she knows he uses pornography. The first few times this happened, I asked Celestia how in the world she could know this after watching or interacting with him for mere minutes. She would say, "I can feel it and see it in how detached he is, in how he looks at women, and how I feel in his presence." Early on, I would sometimes remark that this seemed to be a rather harsh and premature conclusion from exceedingly subjective, if not flimsy, evidence. But dozens of times, her hypotheses have subsequently proven true. I have learned to trust her keen instincts. Healthy women often intuitively recognize a disconnected and objectifying glance.[26] Pornography impacts men far more than men can imagine.

---

24. One of the most sobering aspects of depravity is the human capacity to completely deaden the conscience and harden the heart so that increasingly egregious sins can be committed with emotional ease; cf. Eph 4:18–19; 1 Tim 4:1–2.

25. Zillmann and Bryant, "Pornography's Impact on Sexual Satisfaction."

26. Formal research studies have been conducted demonstrating this reality. For instance, see McKenzie-Mohr and Zanna, "Treating Women as Sexual Objects."

4. Men become increasingly insensitive, unromantic, and aggressive when engaging in sex.

Because pornography conditions men to demean and devalue women and to objectify them for their own instant self-gratification, it influences men to become callous and aggressive when "making love" with their spouse. At the least extreme level, this is evidenced in a lack of kissing, affectionate touching, and foreplay.

5. Men develop a distorted sense of female sexuality and come to believe that women enjoy degrading practices.

Research shows that viewing pornography greatly alters men's sense of normal sexual behavior. They inaccurately believe that most people engage in more extreme sexual practices and that the distorted sex acts they see in pornography are normal and acceptable. In time, they often expect or even demand that their wives engage in these same degrading sexual activities.[27] Often, they seem genuinely surprised and offended that their wives aren't eager to act out their bizarre and humiliating fantasies. We have often heard men berate their wives for being "old-fashioned prudes who hate sex" when, in reality, these brave women value sex too much to allow their husbands to force perverse sex acts upon them. Most often, however, wives feel increasingly insecure and confused about their intimacy needs and become quieter in the marriage. Their survival instinct toward sex is to "just put up with it" rather than deal with it. A wife's silence in this context serves to reinforce the sexual misconceptions of her pornography-using husband. Typically, because of their self-doubt and shame, Christian women tend not to share their emotional and sexual pain with anyone, including other women.

Josephine's story illustrates this tendency. She came to me (Celestia) after her sixtieth birthday. She was in a thirty-five year marriage to a man who did not love her or commit to her. They were both corporate executives working for the same company. She had ignored his chronic "sexual indiscretions." He had come drunk to their wedding. On their honeymoon, he deeply wounded her by his sexual roughness and callousness to her emotional needs. When she began to cry, he became angry and accused her of being crazy. This first conjugal night set the tone for their marriage. Confusingly, her mother loved this charismatic and successful

---

27. Zillmann, "Effects of Prolonged Consumption of Pornography," 127–57; Zillmann and Bryant, "Pornography, Sexual Callousness, and the Trivialization of Rape."

husband and never saw the underbelly of their relationship. Josephine made an unspoken vow of silence to "keep her marriage together." By the time she came to me, she had taken an inventory of what she had lost: her physical health to two sexually transmitted diseases and clinical depression, her financial security (he had spent her family's inheritance to fund his sexual addiction), her spiritual health (she had stopped going to church and pursuing her spirituality in an effort to please him), and her dignity. Telling the truth about her marriage was her first step toward recovery and life. Nothing would change in her marriage until she required it to change.

6. Men often experience greatly diminished libido for their wives.

Men who use pornography often distort and dissipate all of their sexual energy, so they have very little healthy energy for their wives. This dynamic is essentially the reverse of the previous two effects. Satan hates for us to enjoy any of God's exquisite gifts, especially one as beautiful and powerful as marital sex. So, it seems that he doesn't much care which side of the mountain we fall of, as long as we fall off.

7. Men often struggle with physical and emotional impotence.

This is surely one of Satan's most ironic "bait and switch" operations. He seduces men into believing that pornography will help them become more vibrantly sexual, more masculine, and more sexually powerful. However, after they have taken the bait and begun using pornography, they are not only less healthily masculine, but they can no longer demonstrate one of the most basic involuntary biological indicators of adult male sexuality: the ability to maintain an erection. This sexual dysfunction, in turn, further diminishes a man's sense of confident masculinity. Celestia has been a professional counselor for almost two decades working with hundreds of couples. She has been staggered in the past few years by the growing frequency of young married male clients who struggle with intense levels of anxiety and fear in their sexual relationship with their wives. They are often unable to sustain an erection and have difficulty staying focused on their wives during sex. This unprecedented change in her counseling practice is often linked to pornography usage.

IMPACT OF PORNOGRAPHY ON WIVES/GIRLFRIENDS [28]

Pornography impacts the female partners of men who use it in a myriad of ways; these are the ones I (Celestia) find most notable:

1. BROKEN TRUST.

Research studies reveal that a high percentage of women who discover their partner is using pornography feel a great sense of betrayal. Though their husband or boyfriend has not actually had sexual contact with others, these women view their partner's pornographic activities as a form of infidelity. They experience great distress that "the man has taken the most intimate aspect of the relationship, sexuality, which is supposed to express the bond of love between the couple and be confined exclusively to the relationship, and shared it with countless fantasy women."[29] Based on Jesus' words in Matthew 5:28, "Everyone who looks at a woman with lust has already committed adultery with her in his heart." Pornography usage is a form of infidelity. These women rightly feel betrayed. Since trust is foundational to intimacy, this is one of the most damaging effects of pornography upon a spouse.

2. WOMEN EXPERIENCE A SIGNIFICANT SENSE OF PERSONAL REJECTION AND FEELINGS OF PROFOUND SHAME.

Women whose partners use pornography experience its impact daily, even if they are unaware of their husband's usage. They feel their husbands' lack of respect, emotional disengagement, lack of relationally focused sexual energy, and the chronic absence of tender affection and selfless love. When women discover that their husbands are using pornography, they are typically shattered with overwhelming feelings of rejection and personal inadequacy. These destructive experiences typically create deep levels of toxic shame.

---

28. It should be noted that both men and women use pornography, but due to the limited scope of this book, we will be focusing primarily on the deleterious relational effects of a man's use of pornography on his partner or spouse. Current research shows that one-third of online consumers of pornography are female. An excellent personal account of the impact of pornography by a Christian wife is given by Hall, *An Affair of the Mind*.

29. Bergner and Bridges, "The Significance of Heavy Pornography Involvement"; Schneider, "Effects of Cybersex Addiction."

3. Women typically feel responsible for their husbands' sexual disinterest and, therefore, believe themselves to blame.

Wives whose husbands use pornography innately conclude that they must not be "good enough" or their husband wouldn't "need to go elsewhere." For example, I have had many beautiful clients choose to enhance their breasts surgically after sexual and emotional betrayal by husbands who were self-proclaimed sex addicts. A real woman will always feel "less than" in comparison to pornographic images depicting perfectly air-brushed women with surgically enhanced breasts on unnaturally thin bodies. Sadly, not only are women not validated for the relational distress that pornography causes, but they are often told by sex therapists, advice columnists, and even counselors to "stop complaining and learn to understand their man." In other words, they are somehow to blame.

4. Women feel intense pressure to accommodate pornography's perverse messages.

A woman reasons that, if she gives a man what he is looking for, he won't have a need for pornography. The problem with this is that pornography glorifies the practices that healthy women are least likely to accommodate, e.g., "facials" (his ejaculation in her face), anal sex, oral sex as sex, watching pornography together as part of foreplay, etc. The pressure women feel can overwhelm their God-given, healthy sensual desires. Paula Rinehart, in her book *Sex and the Soul of a Woman,* describes this innate female knowing: "Something in us knows that a woman's throat wasn't made to be a receptacle for a man—that it degrades her, that it cheapens the real experience."[30] Our sexuality, as expressed in our marriages, is an echo of the larger story of Christ's love for us and our response to him. We are women created in God's image. Within our soul, we know what we are made for: the safe and committed love of a godly man.[31] Pornography can coerce women to ignore and short-circuit this healthy inner voice, and thus accommodate destructive messages and practices.

30. Rinehart, *Sex and the Soul of a Woman,* 103.

31. When I speak of a godly man, I am specifically referring to a man who knows how to love his wife as "Christ loved the church and gave himself up for her" (Eph 5:25).

5. WOMEN FEEL OVERWHELMED AND POWERLESS TO DO ANYTHING ABOUT THE EFFECTS OF PORNOGRAPHY IN THEIR RELATIONSHIPS.

We believe this is a result of the various influences around them. For instance, many adult women grew up with mothers who told them, "Boys will be boys." These young women grew up experiencing the effects of profound denial from their own mothers, who dismissed all kinds of sexually perverted behavior within the home. A common example of this is when a wife will overlook her husband's pornography, only to have her own children exposed to it within their home. These young boys and girls grow up to be adults programmed to "look the other way." Satan has created a culture of silence that entombs and perpetuates this poison even in Christian homes.

6. OVER TIME, PORNOGRAPHY CAN CREATE A GATEWAY INTO LESBIAN RELATIONSHIPS.

Several of the women I (Celestia) have counseled had transitioned into lesbian relationships to escape the demeaning and destructive roles they were being asked to play in their relationships with men. They felt completely powerless to create a relationship with a man in which they would receive the level of respect they longed for and were designed for. So, they sadly met a legitimate need (love, affection, being treated as an equal) in the only way that felt safe and viable.

Shift #3: Prosperity-Fed Narcissism

Many in "first-world" countries live in the most prosperous cultures in the history of human civilization. We have virtually unlimited choices and resources. While most who share our planet are living at a subsistence level, struggling to obtain adequate nutrition, water, housing, and basic medical care, many of us have the luxury of focusing not on our *needs,* but on our *wants.* The more we have, the more we want. Furthermore, the broader first-world global culture has fed our obsession with ourselves. For instance, a common advertising strategy is to pitch a given product as one we "richly deserve." In our materially blessed culture, we become accustomed to high-quality, readily available products. And, if we don't like a product we have purchased, we can get our money back and choose another, for, in affluent cultures, "the customer is king." We enjoy bountiful legal rights. If our rights are violated, we can sue, and possibly win thousands of dollars or Euros in compensation. We have become so accustomed to special treatment that we subtly come to believe that it is what we are due, what we are entitled to.

Having traveled and ministered in many other cultures, including some of the most impoverished, we are thankful for the legal protection and rights enjoyed in the United States and other developed nations. However, our material and legal blessings have made us increasingly self-absorbed and narcissistic.

For example, a team of five researchers recently surveyed more than 16,000 college students across the United States to assess the narcissism of the current state of the "me generation." Utilizing a standardized assessment tool for narcissism, the researchers found that two-thirds of college students surveyed in 2008 had above-average scores for narcissism, which was a 30 percent increase since 1982, when a similar study was conducted.[32] The researchers warned that, while narcissism may be helpful for getting an audition on *American Idol,* it seriously undermines our ability to experience healthy relationships.[33] In the unvarnished world of real human connection, we won't always be king, our friends won't have all the qualities we want, and our deeply cherished rights will be at times ignored and occasionally violated.

Our financial and technological prosperity can also threaten our relationships by creating unrealistic expectations. Barry Schwartz, author of *The Paradox of Choice,* notes that an overload of choice can make us question the decisions we make before we even make them, and can foster "unrealistically high expectations."[34] Unrealistic expectations are particularly harmful to intimacy, for they not only hamper our ability to build healthy relationships, but can also keep us from enjoying them when we have them. Interesting research suggests that the "happiness level" in one's brain (dopamine levels) depends less on the experience itself than on one's *expectations* regarding that experience.[35] The higher and more unrealistic the expectations, the lower the sense of satisfaction and happiness when the reality of that relationship is experienced. To put it positively, the more realistic our expectations are for our partner, the better our chances are of experiencing regular bursts of dopamine during regular (real-life) experiences with that partner. In summary,

32. Twenge et al., "Egos Inflating Over Time."
33. Crary, "Study—College Students More Narcissistic."
34. Schwartz, *The Paradox of Choice,* 3.
35. Johnson, *Mind Wide Open,* 152.

during the course of a relationship, if we are expecting perfection, we will be disappointed and angry when parts of the real, imperfect person begin to emerge. Essentially, the more romanticized and idealized our expectations, the more noncommittal we become.[36]

This side of heaven, we will never meet a perfect person. Often, we simply don't know what others' flaws and warts are, but, rest assured, they exist. This principle can be particularly challenging for adults who have been single for a long time. Ironically, just as time often increases our desire for a mate, it can also intensify our expectations and decrease our willingness to compromise our vision of a perfect partner. Compounding this dynamic is the fact that, often, with each failed relationship comes a longer checklist for the "perfect" partner who is out there somewhere.

Shift #4: Fragmented and Impersonal

From the day of Adam and Eve's first sin until now, building healthy relationships has been challenging for people of every culture. We are all sinners with an innate propensity toward self-protection and self-interest. But, since we are also made in the image of God, every family and culture also expresses varying degrees of positive relational qualities, such as kindness to strangers, sacrificial loyalty to friends and family, respect for women, compassion and kindness toward those with mental and physical handicaps, etc. Families and cultures that place high value on relationships give children both a script (innate skills) and examples to follow. Unfortunately, cultural changes in the United States and elsewhere in the past several decades have often created fewer experiences and examples of healthy relationships. We live in an increasingly impersonal and fragmented culture.

The corporate environment, for example, has become increasingly cold and utilitarian. We recently read of a major new industrial trend—outsourcing employee firing to paid consultants who come in to a company for a few hours to inform an employee whom they have never met that the company has fired them. The consultant then ushers the terminated employee off the property once and for all. The fired employee cannot have a final conversation with his or her coworkers or supervisor.

---

36. Florence Falk, telephone interview with Jillian Strauss as recorded in *Unhooked Generation*, 39–40.

Not only is the workplace more impersonal and relationally unhealthy, so are our families. Since 1970, divorce rates have quadrupled, and the number of couples cohabiting has risen almost 450 percent. As children of divorce grow up and become parents themselves, they lack "scripts" for marital health and, hence, are more likely to also have marriages end in divorce. Finally, young adults' sexual practices also condition them against intimacy. In the past decade, we have witnessed the development of the "hookup" phenomenon. "Hooking up" is a deliberately ambiguous phrase that connotes any sexual activity between two people who have little or no commitment. Thus, they can "unhook" easily, because there is no romantic involvement. One journalist who investigated this phenomenon notes that it reflects a major cultural shift in which young adults "have virtually abandoned dating and replaced it with group get-togethers and sexual behaviors that are detached from love or commitment—and sometimes even from liking. . . . Sex is becoming the primary currency of social interaction."[37]

These cultural changes have left young adults with a sense of ambivalent pessimism regarding relationships in general and marriage in particular. Secular journalist Jillian Strauss conducted in-depth interviews with more than one hundred single men and women in their twenties and thirties to assess their relational styles, experiences, and beliefs. She published her findings in a fascinating book entitled *Unhooked Generation: The Truth about Why We're Still Single*. Strauss cogently argues that her generation of young adults, from childhood to early adulthood, have witnessed and experienced so many failed relationships that they have developed a "pessimism paradox." Those she interviewed "desperately wanted a lifelong bond, but at the same time, they expressed serious doubts that marriage could ever supply this bond for them."[38] This is precisely what we heard recently when we taught a class on relationships at our seminary. We vividly remember one student's face the last night of class. He came up to us after the students had left and said, "Dr. Tracy, Julie and I can't thank you and Celestia enough for this class. You are the first couple we have ever met who has given us a positive example of marriage. We both come from broken homes, both of us had parents who cheated on each other, we stumbled through our single years making all kinds of painful mistakes, and we were frankly clueless about

37. Stepp, *Unhooked*, 4.
38. Strauss, *Unhooked Generation*, 161.

how to build an intimate marriage. You have given us hope—especially by being so honest about your own failures and struggles and what God has taught you about marriage." While we appreciated his gratitude, it deeply grieves us that we were the first positive marital example this young couple had known.

The alarming news is that, since Adam and Eve left the garden of Eden, intimacy has been disrupted for all of us. Our sin natures, Satan, and the imperfect cultures in which we live make lifelong intimacy seem much like the legend of King Arthur in Camelot—a beautiful and enticing fable of a faraway land that no longer exists. In spite of these doubts, we must continue to embrace the radically good news: that the awesome, eternal God of the universe is incomprehensibly intimate and has made us in his image so that we might enjoy splendid, thirst-quenching intimacy with him and each other. This God-given intimacy can be our God-given reality if we follow his blueprint.

PART TWO

Creating Intimacy
The Art of Bonding

3

God's Blueprint

Because we have our own pride, after all. We make our own way in the world, we fight our own battles, We are not looking for any handouts, We do not want something for nothing. It threatens our self-esteem, our self-reliance. And because to accept such a gift from another would be to bind us closer to him than we like to be bound to anybody. And maybe most of all because if another man dies so that I can live, it imposes a terrible burden on my life. From that point on, I cannot live any longer just for myself. . . . My debt to Him is so great that the only way I can approach paying it is by living a life as brave and beautiful as his death. . . . I can only live my life for what it truly is: Not a life that is mine by natural right, to live anyway that I choose, But a life that is mine only because he gave it to me, And I have got to live it in a way that he also would have chosen.

—Frederick Buechner[1]

OUR ORIGINAL AND ETERNAL DANCE

WE ARE CREATED FOR real intimacy, with a profound core desire to feel "felt" and understood, to know and be known in safe relationship. We simultaneously long for this kind of connection and are terrified of it. We reach for others and then subtly push them away. In our fragile humanity, we have hurt and been hurt; many of us have made fierce determinations never to be hurt again. Consciously or subconsciously, we vow, "I will not be vulnerable to anyone." These are natural defenses to early and chronic rejections by those who gave us life, which can lead

1. Buechner, *Listening to Your Life,* 145–46.

to chronically low self-esteem, anxiety, and intense relational fears. We are pummeled with intolerable reminders of our disappointment to God and others; we secretly wonder if we will ever know real intimacy.

In spite of these personal doubts, God offers us radically "good news." He is the One who initiates toward us a knowing and intimate relationship. Intimacy, then, is not ours to figure out, but instead ours for the taking—or, more accurately, ours for the surrendering. God initiates first. His bold and penetrating love knows the best and worst of who we are, and yet still desires relationship with us. His love redeems us from the shame and self-knowledge of all that is wrong in us. As we grow and are able to absorb and surrender to his initiating, unconditional love, we begin to experience a freedom and joy in that love. Brennan Manning insightfully depicts God's voice to us:

> Did you know that every time you tell me you love me, I say thank you? . . . Were you grieved by the divine command to Abraham that he slay his only begotten Isaac on Mount Moriah? Were you relieved when the angel intervened and Abraham's hand was stayed, and the sacrifice was not carried out? Have you forgotten that on Good Friday no angel intervened? That sacrifice was carried out, and it was my heart that was broken. Are you aware that I had to raise Jesus from the dead on Easter morning because my love is everlasting? Are you serenely confident that I will raise you too, my adopted child?[2]

This is how we can begin to feel worthy and enjoyed, not because of who we are and what we have done, but because we are intimately, individually, and passionately loved by a perfect and beautiful Father King. In other words, as sinful people, we are not loved by God because we are beautiful; rather, we are beautiful because we are loved by God.[3] His love creates beauty and worth in us. Thus, we can feel worthy when we see ourselves reflected in his eyes. The more we surrender and absorb his love for us, the more vulnerable and honest we can be about our true selves, especially the weak, needy, broken, and angry parts of ourselves. As we grow in our intimacy with God, we can begin to hold our heads high based on his grace and unrelenting love of us. This gives us the strength and boldness to risk entering into intimate connection with

2. Manning, *The Ragmuffin Gospel,* 166–67.
3. Bloesch, *God the Almighty,* 151–52.

others, in spite of the fact that they cannot, or will not, ever be able to love us perfectly.

Furthermore, God's love for us activates a response of love in us—a desire to give back to him.[4] Service to our King, then, is not done out of duty, but out of delight![5] There are times in which I am so overcome by my heavenly Father's patient love of me that I feel as if I cannot give enough of myself back to him. I long to give him all of me. This is our first eternal dance of intimacy that will form the basis for every other relationship, if we pay attention to the notes.

Because we bear the image of our Creator, from the moment of our conception forward, we are made to experience intimacy with God as well as others. Shawn Mullins captures this mystery in his poetic song, *Shimmer:*

> He's born to shimmer, he's born to shine
> He's born to radiate
> He's born to live, he's born to love.

Our first experience of human intimacy begins within our mother's womb. Desmond Morris, a secular anthropologist who spent a lifetime studying the biological aspects of human intimacy, beautifully describes our earliest experiences of life: "floating in a warm fluid, curling inside a total embrace, swaying to the undulations of the moving body and hearing the beat of the pulsing heart. Our prolonged exposure to these . . . leaves a lasting impression on our brains, an impression that spells security, comfort and passivity."[6] We believe that this nine-month intrauterine impression of safety, love, presence, and provision by another congruently echoes the eternal love embrace of our heavenly Father. In a sense, we have the ideal of perfect intimacy scripted into our very souls. Drawing on biblical tradition, Philip Newell describes the imprinting of creation and the effects of the fall:

> Our deepest place of identity is the beauty of Eden. The Genesis
> picture is not of the garden being destroyed but rather of Adam
> and Eve moving into a type of exile from it. Eden, of course, is
> not a place from which we are distant in space and time. Rather,

4. 2 Cor 5:14; cp. Jude 21.

5. For a wonderful treatment of delighting in Christ as the overarching goal of the Christian life, in contrast to serving Christ out of mere duty, see Piper, *Desiring God*.

6. Morris, *Intimate Behaviour,* 15.

it is a dimension within ourselves from which we have become separated. Like Adam and Eve we have become fugitives from the beauty of our origins . . . our beauty is distorted. It has been covered over and blighted by wrongdoing and sin.[7]

The infant's cry upon birth bears testimony to the human terror of losing this physical and intimate connection with another human being. The loving embrace of the mother's arms soon replaces the rhythmic embrace of the womb. At this time, the baby's most comforting embrace is to be wrapped in a way that allows for as much bodily contact as possible.

As we write, I (Celestia) am remembering the birth of our first daughter. We had nervously and impatiently waited to meet her officially, and finally that day arrived. We were whisked into the delivery room and, within hours, she was on her way! Following a raucous announcement of her disapproval concerning the sudden and rude environmental changes she was experiencing, Dr. Sargeant promptly placed her into my arms. As he did, I knew instinctively what to do—and so did she. I reached for her, wrapping my arms around her tiny body and pulled her to my chest. My visceral responses to her wail came from a deeply organic place within my soul. As I comforted her, I wasn't following a manual or class outline, but instead was intuitively responding to her cries for comfort out of a deeply buried love song within. As I held her, she would startle or cry and I would instinctively comfort her by rocking and humming softly until she was settled again. This early relational exchange felt like a warm and symbiotic dance—natural and automatic. Hours later, our beautiful daughter was offered my breast for sucking and nourishment. Her need for warmth and the sweetness of this early nourishing and comforting touch would be repeated in various other forms later in adult contexts.[8]

During this initial stage of postuterine life, the infant's cry elicits human comfort and contact. Morris goes on to describe how such crying begins in a tearless way. However, full weeping quickly develops only three to four weeks after birth. Later, in an adult, this weeping can occur separately, by itself, or as a silent signal. Do you know that we are the only species of God's creation that weeps? Tears are visible signals that glisten and trickle conspicuously. What is a healthy mother's response? She dries the eyes of her baby—another soothing act of bodily contact.

7. Newell, *Echo of the Soul*, 61.

8. Morris, *Intimate Behaviour*, 25.

Morris suggests that the human mother has a strong drive to clean her infant. Therefore, tears are a powerful behavior that stimulates a comforting response at times of emotional distress. Tears also serve a biological function—they clean and protect the eyes. However, full weeping serves a purely social function. Both smiling and crying are subtle encouragements for intimacy. These built-in prompters for nurture and attention are especially important for the human infant, since a baby does not have the ability to hold on to the mother for its survival like other primates. As human beings, we are dependent throughout our lifespan on others to hold on to us not only for survival, but for our very identity.

By the third and fourth month of life, new patterns of bodily contact appear in the form of reflexes. Soon, the automatic grasp and moro (startle) reflex disappear and are replaced by intentional and directed grasping and clinging. The infant can now coordinate eyes and hands and refines hugging by six months of age. The baby soon begins to replace holding with an increased sensitivity to emotional and visual communication. Throughout the first year of life, contact with the mother can operate well at a distance, often without words.

In the third year of life, with the acquisition of a foundational vocabulary, verbal contact is added to the child's ability to connect visually and emotionally. Now, feelings can also be expressed and received through words. As the child grows, there will be an ongoing need for bodily contact and emotional intimacy which will take on varied forms throughout the child's development. Consider, as an example, the rough-and-tumble play of early childhood. Fathers are often best at this type of bodily contact and, to a mother's surprise, prefer it as a bedtime activity!

Another example that comes to mind of these developing and ever-evolving physical/emotional/verbal connections comes from a series of memories of our son as an early adolescent. While in junior high, Luke would sometimes come home from school after a particularly stressful day, feeling sullen and agitated. He typically would not be in the mood to converse, and would instead bound up the stairs to his room. Later in the evening after dinner, I would slip into his room and sit beside his bed—quietly rubbing his back. This would often be the best time for us to connect. It's as if my appropriate physical touch stimulated an emotional and verbal response from him and thus facilitated a deeper connection between us. Today, some of our best memories come from this intentional time of being together.

Adolescence is the final stage of the child's development. By this time, the intimacy patterns have changed several times. With teens, brief intimacies with parents still take place such as a peck on the cheek, greetings, and farewells. However, the push in adolescence is toward increased privacy, independence, and a relational focus outside the home. As the child continues to mature toward independence, he or she will arrive at post-adolescence and typically move outside the family. For the young adult and his or her family, a second birth has been experienced: "The womb of the family is abandoned as was the womb of the mother two decades before."[9]

As this young adult enters into his or her own intimate relationship, the intimacy sequence begins again.

> For Adam no suitable helper was found. So the Lord God caused the man to fall into a deep sleep; and while he was sleeping, he took one of the man's ribs and closed up the place with flesh. Then the Lord God made a woman from the rib he had taken out of the man, and he brought her to the man. The man said, "This is now bone of my bones and flesh of my flesh; she shall be called 'woman,' for she was taken out of man." (Gen 2:22–23 NIV)

This sequence moves providentially on, ideally copying the first securely attached parent/child relationship. The biblical creation account anticipates this relational movement: "For this reason a man will leave his father and mother and be united to his wife, and they will become one flesh" (Gen 2:24). Marriage marks the beginning of our second human love story—man and woman in intimate relationship with each other.

A MODEL FOR BUILDING INTIMACY IN A FRACTURED WORLD

> A virtual epidemic of "care-less-ness" threatens to de-civilize modern societies. . . . Over and against these trends toward individualism, isolation, inhumanity, and uncivility stands the biblical word that it is not good for individuals to be alone. Our God intends that we live in community; that we be each other's keepers. People are not meant to contend with loneliness, emotional

9. Ibid., 33.

distance from one another, and destructive relationships. We are created for fellowship; in a word, we are born to bond.[10]

Our Intimacy Journey

We are often asked, "Where did you get your intimacy model?" This book is the fuller answer to that question. It reflects our story and the monumental transformation that was woven into the structure of our love. We began our relationship a lot like other Christian couples, birthed into the center of the conservative, traditional church. We met in high school and married before graduating from college. We knew we were headed for church ministry, so we promptly enrolled in seminary to complete this final leg of preparation. We were wild and starry-eyed in our love for each other and our desire to serve God together. We had an idea that two would definitely be better than one, but were quite naïve to the process God had in store for us.

Midwinter of 1983, I (Celestia) had a catastrophic skiing accident that precipitated a series of extensive orthopedic surgeries and hospitalizations. I was just twenty-five years old at the time. Steve was serving as a youth pastor and was a full-time seminary student. Before my accident, our schedules were full, and our days were neatly structured. We had certainly not factored a debilitating injury and multiple surgeries into our early years of marriage. In a few short minutes, on the icy slopes of Mt. Hood, our well-ordered lives came screeching to an abrupt halt. I was rudely and indefinitely "benched." Needless to say, this unexpected turn of events knocked our world upside down. We had no way of knowing then that this was just the beginning. This initial orthopedic emergency would be the first of seventeen subsequent major surgeries I would undergo in the ensuing twenty-seven years—approximately one every fifteen or sixteen months.[11] As you can imagine, our roles and responsibilities within our marriage briskly changed. Our old models were inadequate for the years ahead.

Until this accident, we had been very busy for God. I covered every home and parenting need while Steve worked outside the home. I was efficient, organized, and relationally independent. I worked very hard to

10. Joy, *Bonding*, 9.

11. Celestia was eventually diagnosed with an autoimmune disease, which helped explain her body's reluctance to heal.

need as little from Steve as possible, because, after all, it felt as if I were competing with God. It felt selfish to take Steve's time and energy away from his God-ordained ministries for my needs. I performed faithfully— for God, Steve, and the church. Our model had so much "polish" to it that it was questioned by no one—including ourselves. We were forced, by the loving and sovereign hand of God, to alter almost every paradigm and practice we had brought into our marriage.

I found myself no longer able to assist Steve or anybody else. I was doing well most days just to get out of bed. I battled a lingering depression that I could not name, shake, or understand. The world as I knew it had changed forever. What we could not have known at the time was that, as a result of these abrupt life-altering disruptions, God was silently creating new relational patterns of love that Steve and I practice and teach today. God opened up for us beautiful moments of intimacy, not only with each other, but also with him, that have become the rhythm of our love and our marriage—the breath of our love.

Brennan Manning describes a similar life transformation when he heard Christ speaking to him: "For love of you, I left my Father's side. I came to you who ran from me, who fled me, who did not want to hear my name. For love of you I was covered with spit, punched, and beaten, and fixed to the wood of the cross." Manning's commentary on this experience is instructive. He states "[O]nce you come to know the love of Jesus Christ, nothing else in the world will seem as beautiful or desirable."[12] We can only experience this intimate, redeeming presence of God when we have come to the end of ourselves, recognizing and acknowledging our utter brokenness and, therefore, our desperate need of a loving, redeeming Lord.

> God is, in one way or another, trying to get messages through our blindness as we move around down here, knee-deep in the fragrant muck of misery and marvel of the world. It is not objective proof of God's existence that we want, but the experience of God's presence. That is the miracle we are really after, and that is also, I think, the miracle that we really get.[13]

God invites us into the same kind of love that he demonstrated toward us. Human value and dignity are most fully realized in healthy

---

12. Manning, Official Home Page.

13. Buechner, *The Magnificent Defeat*, 47.

relationship. If we are left completely alone, solitude and isolation cast shadows over our sense of worthiness. This is why God made us for intimate relationships. Walter Wangerin, in his very transparent book on marriage, acknowledges the profound way God communicates to us through others, particularly our spouse: "Lacking companions at the level of the soul, I finally cannot find my soul. It always takes another person to show myself to me. Alone, I die."[14] Thankfully, our merciful God does not want his children to die. He redirects them to paths of life and uses others to be his instruments of healing.

The relentless medical and physical needs I could not escape forced me to let Steve in. God held me in place, literally, by my body's brokenness, so that I had to receive both God's help and Steve's help for my daily sustenance. It was a most humbling position, but, relationally, it transformed us both. As God began to "rain his righteousness"[15] down upon me, I began to soak in his mercy, and the feelings of toxic shame around my authentic and very flawed self began to heal.

I was beginning to tolerate the reality of my circumstances and to let myself feel all that was happening to me. I could not run from myself or from this process. God taught me to feel deeply and fully—to look for his gifts hidden in pain. To not fear the erratic waves of suffering and loss that coursed over me, often unexpected and always unwanted. I was learning to allow the sorrow to come, like an engulfing ocean's wave—surging, ebbing, and washing my soul. Living with chronic physical pain became my heart's tutor for learning to live with the psychological pain of loss and disappointment. What was my gift in all of this? I began to know the sweetness of Jesus' love, comfort, and mercy—the experience of his presence. Without realizing it, the deeper, subterranean levels of my soul were being healed of the shame that was buried there. In the beginning, I could not receive Steve's merciful care without a rush of embarrassment and shame. As shame surged, God healed. Shame was my blight, not my essence—it did not belong to me.

I desperately needed a new identity, soul-deep, constructed upon the image of God within me. Without my ability to perform for others, I had nothing left that supported my value—my ability to *do* for others had been stripped away and I was left with an emptiness that felt like death. I was in the middle of an inescapable double bind: I felt unworthy

14. Wangerin, *As For Me and My House,* 58.
15. Hos 10:12 (NKJV).

of Steve's selfless care of me, yet, physically, I was dependent upon it. I understand today that God was determined to overwhelm me with his love—even if it meant sitting on me! I had too much self-defensive pride for anyone's love to break through. I was forced to surrender to God's love first, then to Steve's, with nothing to offer back. I was truly the pauper—receiving gifts from the prince and his King.

I resonate with Henri Nouwen, in his life-altering book, *The Return of the Prodigal Son*, when he describes the "lostness" of the dutiful elder brother in this well-known parable of Jesus:

> His lostness is much harder to identify. After all, he did all the right things. He was obedient, dutiful, law-abiding, and hard-working. People respected him, admired him, praised him, and likely considered him a model son. Outwardly, the elder son was faultless. But when confronted by his father's joy at the return of his younger brother, a dark power erupts in him and boils to the surface. Suddenly, there becomes glaringly visible a resentful, proud, unkind, selfish person, one that had remained deeply hidden, even though it had been growing stronger and more powerful over the years. . . . Looking deeply into myself and then around me at the lives of other people, I wonder which does more damage, lust or resentment? There is so much resentment among the "just" and the "righteous." There is so much judgment, condemnation, and prejudice among the "saints." There is so much frozen anger among the people who are so concerned about avoiding "sin."[16]

Perhaps the truest prodigals are those of us who distance ourselves from "sinners" and ultimately from God himself, through our pride and self-righteousness. Thankfully, God found this prodigal and was leading her back to his house of joy.

A Myth Retold

"The secret to enjoying the perfect relationship is simply finding the perfect person, your waiting-to-be-discovered 'soul mate.'" This is perhaps the most widespread relational myth of our day. It appeals to intuitive logic, is reinforced by hundreds of contemporary movies and songs, and provides a thoroughly positive explanation for our relational woes. If we are not enjoying a deeply fulfilling romantic relationship, we simply have

16. Nouwen, *The Return of the Prodigal Son*, 71.

not yet met Mr. or Miss Right. But take heart! Tomorrow may be the day we bump into this person and life will be instantly and magically transformed. This myth is much like the idea of becoming rich by winning the lottery. Instead of the daily discipline of exercising financial restraint and making sound investments month after month, year after year, one can create instant wealth by simply purchasing the winning ticket.

In reality, healthy relationships and soul-satisfying intimacy, much like financial wealth, come from daily discipline and sound relational choices over the course of time. In other words, great relationships are not simply "discovered"; they are slowly and skillfully built.

Stages of Bonding

In section two, we will develop our model of bonding. This model draws heavily upon the work of many who have gone before us and have influenced our understanding and framework for relationships. It also draws from the insights God has given us—two feisty firstborns, committed to the development of our own marital "soul bond." Today, we continue to live and love alongside countless other men and women who share the same longing and desperation for real intimacy as we do.

Desmond Morris, in his classic study, *Intimate Behaviour,* explains that twelve identifiable stages of bonding have been discovered in studies of human relationships conducted in various cultures.[17] These stages explain how a pair-bond begins, develops, and is sexually consummated. These stages correspond to the relational sequence laid down in Genesis 2 and provide a useful, practical model for the development of an exclusive, bonded relationship experienced within the sacred context of covenantal marriage.

It is most encouraging to know that we *do* have a roadmap for this mysterious journey. For those who have experienced a series of healthy, satisfying relationships, the process of building healthy intimacy is internalized and relatively intuitive. However, for most of us, this is not the case. For many, early family relationships did not reflect unconditional love, nurture, and secure attachments. This distorted mirror shattered the relational pathway and paved the way for strained and broken relationships. Worse yet, many have known the bitter and shaming experiences of betrayal, abuse, or abandonment at the hands of those entrusted with

17. Morris, *Intimate Behaviour,* 72–78.

their protection and care. For the multitude of people who find relationships confusing and frustrating, this section is for you.

Following is an overview of our intimacy model, which includes three distinct dimensions of bonding. These are built upon a spiritual foundation of shared faith, trust, and obedience to God's pathways. Sexual intercourse, then, making love, is the natural and beautiful expression of bonded and committed love within the marriage itself. When a couple delays their sexual experience and expression until after their sacred and public commitment of marital love—the vow of love itself—their sexual intimacy serves as a relational glue chemically super-boosting their bond of love.

The following four chapters describe three distinct stages of bonding. We found that Morris's twelve stages follow a sequential order that fits nicely into our intimacy model. These stages are best understood through interaction with another specific person. The exercises and questions for discussion that follow each stage will guide the reader through the four dimensions: emotional, relational, physical, and sexual. If you are reading this book as a couple, we suggest that you take your time as you move through the sequence, allowing for adequate processing of the material. The questions and exercises will gently lead you into a more intimate connection, helping you to strengthen and deepen your intimacy with each other. The steps are sequential and meant to be followed in the order in which they are presented. The Intimacy Quotients, found in the appendix, will also help you assess your strengths and weaknesses within each of the four dimensions. We suggest that you complete the quotient for each dimension *before* reading the chapter, as it will give you some feedback on your general relational health in a particular dimension. It is our desire that this book and these tools give you not only a practical guide for deepened intimacy, but also serve as a resource for assessing the health of your current relationship.

Following are Morris's twelve stages of bonding, placed within the four primary dimensions of intimacy:

Emotional: The Language of the Heart
Stage One: Eye to Body
Stage Two: Eye to Eye
Stage Three: Voice to Voice

Relational: The Art of Cherishing
Stage Four: Hand to Hand
Stage Five: Arm to Shoulder
Stage Six: Arm to Waist

Physical: The Power of Touch
Stage Seven: Face to Face
Stage Eight: Hand to Head
Stage Nine: Hand to Body

Sexual: Love's Magnificent Expression
Stage Ten: Mouth to Breast
Stage Eleven: Hand to Genital
Stage Twelve: Genital to Genital

4

Emotional Dimension

The Language of the Heart

I was in love once. I think love is a bit of heaven. When I was
in love I thought about a girl so much I felt like I was going to
die and it was beautiful, and she loved me. We were not about
ourselves, we were about each other. . . . When I was in love there
was somebody in the world who was more important than me,
and given all that happened at the fall of man, is a miracle, like
something God forgot to curse.

—Donald Miller.[1]

THE FIRST DIMENSION OF bonding is *emotional intimacy—the ability
to both feel and respectfully express our honest feelings to another and
have them understood and validated.* Emotional intimacy creates relational safety. Steve is the one who really knows me—my darkest secrets,
fears, and weaknesses. He knows my history, compulsions, and most
vulnerable needs. I have the security of being myself with him. He both
knows and loves the real Celestia and has the ability to communicate
his understanding and love for me with and without words. This kind of
communication is a language of the heart. Sometimes it is spoken, and
sometimes it is just felt.

Verbal communication comprises the words we use in conversation. Our mere words make up less than 10 percent of the messages we
give to each other. As you can see, our nonverbal communication holds
the most power over our relationships. Nonverbal communication is expressed through facial gestures, posture, eye contact, hand gestures, pace,

1. Miller, *Blue Like Jazz*, 151.

intensity, and tone of voice. Through our emotional communication, we are constantly conveying and receiving one of three primary messages: "I care about you and what you are saying to me," "I do not care about you," or "I am ambivalent or apathetic toward you." Often, we are not aware of the messages we convey, especially to those we love. Our words may be communicating one message while 93 percent of our nonverbal communication is conveying something else. Relationships that are emotionally intimate have a feedback loop—a pathway for communicating to our partner (who listens and cares) our concerns regarding our relationship.

We will now address the first three stages of bonding that fit within the emotional dimension. We suggest that each stage be completed before moving on to the next. The questions and exercises that follow each stage will serve as a relational guide for you as a couple as you practice the art of emotional communication. As a reader, take your time as you move through this sequence. Make time for an actual exchange of ideas, feelings, and thoughts. If you are reading this book as a couple, consider using these stages as a simple assessment of the current quality of your relational bond. For instance, if you are kissing as a couple, but have not learned to share honestly with each other or to resolve conflict well, you have skipped several crucial steps of bonding and would be best served to stop kissing and back the relationship up to the earlier stages until they are mastered. If you are reading this book as a single, these steps will also serve as a guide in the formation of a satisfying and intimate relationship.

There are four Intimacy Quotients in the back of this book. They are to be filled out before reading the next four chapters and may serve as a simple assessment of your individual "health" in each of the four dimensions of bonding: emotional, relational, physical, and sexual. There are quotients for both singles and married couples. Complete and score your quotients independently of your partner. We encourage you to finish reading the chapter before sharing them with each other.

Stage One: Eye to Body

This initial stage of relationship is the first glance—the first exciting awareness of another that forms an unforgettable snapshot within the mind. Donald Joy describes these memory photos as leaving chemical tracers in the brain that "block out the rest of the world."[2] This seemingly random pairing ignites our senses in an instant—often without warning. Love does seem "blind," as others will often fail to see what a couple sees in each other. I will never forget observing Steve on our high school campus. He was popular and carried his athletic body with confidence. He enjoyed the respect of his peers, and this showed in the way that he walked. I remember noticing the size of his thighs and muscular calves, his thick coarse brown hair, his square jaw, and the cadence of his step. In crowds, he would hold his head up and slightly back. I could easily distinguish him in a sea of people.

2. Joy, *Bonding,* 43–44.

In this early relational stage, I observed. There was no touch or even words at this point. I was collecting all kinds of information about this extraordinary man. I watched him play football, run track, lead Bible studies, joke with friends, talk to his mother, eat lunch, and study. Without realizing it, we were laying the first step of an emotionally intimate foundation for a future relationship. We liked what we saw in each other, and were ready for the next steps.

Clearly, this early "awareness" is not sexualized or a lustful stare, which would instead be a narcissistic focus on myself and my own experience, apart from him, and would objectify him. As Lilian Berger notes, "The more we practice out-of-context sexuality, the more we lose the ability to practice true intimacy. The more sex becomes a performance."[3] And the more sex becomes a performance, the more disconnected we become from our inner selves and each other, creating a gulf between the self and the body. As this gulf widens, the more compulsive and pleasure-oriented a person becomes to "feel connected." All too easily, this can create "a vicious cycle of drawing near and alienation"[4] which eventually destroys the very foundation needed for intimacy—the longing to give oneself fully to another. Promiscuous, self-focused sexual pleasure results in the complete abandonment of the other person. Therefore, it deadens both our body and soul. Conversely, real intimacy makes the *person within the body*, rather than the *perfection of the body*, the focus. Real intimacy is begun without touch or words. Who are you as you move within your world?

Exercises and Questions for Reflection and Sharing: Eye to Body

1. How did your relationship begin? What did you notice about the other that caused you to be attracted to him/her?

2. Describe your spouse. How does his/her body fill the space around them?

3. Describe the physical (nonsexual) characteristics of your spouse that you are most attracted to. What is unique about him/her?

3. Barger, *Eve's Revenge*, 151.
4. Ibid.

4. When you think of the beginning of your relationship, what are you most thankful for? What do you most regret?

5. When do you feel noticed by your spouse? When are you hurt by him/her "not seeing" you? "Tell me one specific thing I can do to change this."

6. Read Genesis 2:24–25. "In what ways have I not 'left' my parents? How might this affect my 'cleaving' to you?"

7. End this time by holding hands, kneeling by the chair or bed, and praying for each other. Attune your prayers to what you have heard and observed in this time together. Pray for relational protection and strength to follow through with promises made; make bold declarations of your love for God and each other.

Stage Two: Eye to Eye

Neuropsychiatrist Louann Brizendine, in *The Female Brain*, reports that women cry four times more easily than men, "displaying an unmistakable sign of sadness and suffering that men can't ignore."[5] She goes on to describe the elegant capacity of the female brain to scan the human face for nonverbal information accurately and intuitively. Her body and brain are created to receive emotional signals: "This information is sent through her brain circuits to search her emotional memory banks for a match."[6] Is his face tight or relaxed? Does he blink and dart his eyes or make eye contact? Does he clench or relax his jaw? Her eyes and facial muscles will automatically mimic the expressions upon his face. This process is called "mirroring." Her brain will begin to stimulate its own circuits, as if his body sensations and emotions were hers. She does this in the blink of an eye. Because her brain has the automatic capacity to match emotion to event and then to file it into long-term storage, her brain will then be searching for congruency. Are his words consistent

5. Brizendine, *The Female Brain*, 119.
6. Ibid.

with his tone of voice? Or, are his eyes "darting a bit too much for her to believe what he is saying. The meaning of his words, the tone of his voice, and the expression in his eyes do not match. She knows—he is lying."[7] At that moment, all of her systems begin to activate wildly and she goes into "alert."

> Tears are often the telescope by which men see far into heaven.
>
> —Henry Ward Beecher

In contrast, according to many scientists, he is not adept at reading facial expressions (this gender difference has been noted among new-borns and infants with startling consistency[8]) and emotional nuance—especially signs of sadness, despair, or distress. He is relying on her more obvious cues—the tears themselves. He then realizes something is wrong! He often is frustrated that she doesn't know that he loves her, while her chronic complaint is of his emotional insensitivity. "He should just know!" How very important for us to understand our God-designed gender differences (and our individual differences), understanding and validating these in each other.

Sadly, these God-given emotional gifts can be easily numbed in our fragmented, electronic, and sexualized culture—creating even greater emotional and relational disconnection. When we repress our individual emotional connectivity, relationships languish. We can see evidence of emotional repression and numbing in the alarming rise in rates of sexual compulsivity, aggression, and addiction in both men and women.

Let's think again about the vital information communicated through the eyes. As I write, the example that comes readily to mind is the eye contact Steve and I make when we present together. I am often nervous and scanning my environment for reassurances. If, for example, our audience is particularly still and unresponsive, I will glance at Steve and hold eye contact with him. A hundred silent messages are communicated within that blink of time: "Celestia, I love you; I am proud of you; I love doing this with you; you're good . . . you really are; they like what you are saying; I like you to need me; thank you for doing this with me." My brain specifically remembers his eyes. I feel loved and know comfort. At other times, we are together and experiencing something too big or

7. Ibid.

8. J. Connellan et al., "Sex Differences"; Lutchmaya and Baron-Cohen, "Human Sex Differences." For a readable treatment of the neurological basis for the way the male brain recognizes and processes facial gestures and emotions, see Brizendine, *The Male Brain.*

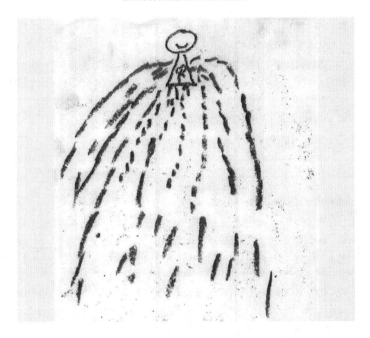

meaningful for words. Our eyes will find each other and I will feel like I am being fed. I am experiencing "presence," and it feels good.

Why do we stop making eye contact? When we decide that our world of relationships is too unsafe, we begin to hide. We conceal our true selves when we stop looking into each other's eyes. In the intimacy of marriage, we are most vulnerable. The drawing above was done by a well known and respected civic leader who depicted her inner pain through tears that fell on the inside of her heart, hidden behind her smile.

I have had countless men and women recollect the specific day in their childhood when they stopped crying. Most often, this occurs in the context of wounds experienced at the hands of those who were entrusted with their care, and in the absence of even one comforter. This moment is often described as their decision to turn a "heart into stone" — a commitment to not feel, trust, or expose their true selves again.[9]

Chronic emotional abandonment (psychological abandonment and abuse can take place in homes that look very good on the outside) or abuse by the parent or guardian who should have been the one offer-

---

9. Contrast this with Ezek 36:26, where God promises to "remove from you your heart of stone and give you a heart of flesh."

ing protection and care results in emotional and relational isolation.[10] Tragically, chronic experiences of abuse and rejection repress the mechanisms God has given for the creation of intimacy. Therefore, it should not be surprising that, as neglect and abuse rates climb, so do patterns of narcissism (pathological absorption and focus on one's self), depression, and addiction—the use of substances to deaden the inner self. In the absence of comforters, there cannot be healing; in the absence of healing, there cannot be safety; in the absence of safety, there cannot be intimacy.

> You have made him exceedingly glad with your presence.
>
> —Psalm 21:6 NKJV

Our gloriously good news is that God preserves within us his original design. Since we image him, he has a vested interest in first redeeming us back to himself in order to heal us, and then in redeeming our relationships with each other. Redemption is the process of bringing life out of death. Our brokenness because of sin—the hurts we have received from others, and the hurts we have perpetrated against others—results in a deadening of our interior selves. Deadening fractures our ability to feel, to connect to our own body, and to trust. Deadening obstructs our vision—we cannot see God's beauty in and around ourselves—and, therefore, we are blocked in experiencing his forgiving presence and reparative love.

Our first healing must be the restoration and connection of our exterior and interior self so that we might experience, with every system of our body and brain, connected intimacy with God, our first and eternal Father—to be able to know and believe in his unconditional love for us. This transforms and redeems our sense of personal value and worth, despite our relational history, because we see ourselves through his eyes as one who is chosen and loved.

> Joy is a mystery because it can happen anywhere, anytime, even under the most uncompromising circumstances, even in the midst of suffering, with tears in its eyes, even nailed to a tree.[11]

This first healing is critical for all of us because we have grown up in a broken world. As children, our first sense of value was the image of

10. Tracy, *Mending the Soul*, 22–37, 100–17.

11. Buechner, *Listening to Your Life*, 287.

ourselves we saw reflected in the eyes of our mother. Was she available, responsive, and comforting? Did she like being with us, or were we a nuisance to be "put up with?" Do we have memories of her comfort, stroking our face or wiping our tears? Did she hurt when we hurt or cry when we cried? How often did she hold us or sit close to us at night? Was she home and available, or distracted and busy with other people and activities? Did we even have a mother, or were we motherless because of death, divorce, neglect, or sickness? The truth for all of us is that there was at least some brokenness in that first human relationship.

God created us in and for Eden—therefore, we search for that *perfect* relationship in which we are unconditionally loved for who we are! Yet, here we sit, clearly not close to anything Edenic, but still wanting to be perfectly known and to know—afraid to trust another because we have been hurt. Isn't it clear, then, that our first healing (knowing and feeling God's delight in us) must take place so that we are freed to live and love others as one who has known *perfect* love? We can then move past our fears of rejection and reluctance to trust, because we have internalized our Father's love of us. Our identity is built, therefore, on our reflection in his eyes!

> My gift to you is love, but worship is your gift to Me.
> And oh, most glorious it is!
> Worship always calls Me "Father" and makes us both rich with common joy.
> Worship Me,
> For only this great gift can set you free from the killing love of self,
> And prick your fear with valiant courage.
> To fly in hope through moments of despair.
> Worship will remind you that no man knows completeness in himself.
> Worship will teach you to speak your name,
> When you've forgotten who you are.
> Worship is duty and privilege,
> Debt and grand inheritance at once.
> Worship, therefore, at those midnights when the stars hide.
> Worship in the storms till love makes thunder whimper and grow quiet
> And listen to your whispered hymns.
> Worship and be free![12]

This first healing is the foundation for the second—the redemption of all that is broken or hurt in our significant relationships. In fact, processing the truth about our childhood, the beauty of what we have

---

12. Miller, *A Requiem for Love*, 18.

enjoyed, and the hurts and abandonments we have survived can become a reparative template for our significant adult relationships. For example, we most need and desire in relationship with our husband or wife what we did not receive as a child. Even the most loving, godly parents are finite, imperfect human beings who have failed and hurt their children in specific ways. Therefore, understanding and connecting with the wounds and vulnerabilities of our family of origin will help us to recognize our adult intimacy needs and intentionally craft our present relationship in healthy ways. To the degree that we are both respectfully honest about our needs and practice a consistent and dependable response to each other, we will we be able to strengthen and deepen our relationship.

In summary, we will be able to love most freely in our adult relationships to the degree that we have acknowledged and healed our earliest relationships. Because we are scripted with strong relational patterns that come out of our families of origin, we will typically recreate these within our adult relationships. As an example, we might risk being attracted to a man or woman who hurts us in some of the same ways we were hurt as a child. Without healing, we might unknowingly and unfeelingly follow the relational scripts we have experienced in the past. The familiar will feel "right."[13] These relational patterns are old worn pathways within the brain that need to be altered!

Early in our relationship, as Steve and I began to share some of our childhood memories with each other, we began to know and understand the unique ways in which we needed to love and be loved in relationship with each other. We began to customize relational guidelines in each of the dimensions of bonding: emotional, relational, and physical (affectionate/nonerotic touch). We cannot love someone well if we do not know his or her scars, the places where they have been deeply hurt. This knowledge guides us in customizing predictable and safe relational responses built upon the desire to love our partner best in the specific places where he or she has been hurt most. These intentional commitments or guidelines then become the template for customizing our love for each other. This healing, and subsequent relational template for intentional love, creates in time an affair-proof marriage.

---

13. Scripture gives many examples of the danger of continuing in unhealthy patterns of past behavior—one's own, and, particularly, that of one's family. Biblically, this is often described as "walking in the sins of the fathers." Cf. Gen 12:13, 20:2, and 26:9; 1 Kgs 15:1–3; 2 Kgs 21:20–22; 2 Chron 30:7; Jer 11:10.

Exercises and Questions for Reflection and Sharing: Eye to Eye

1. Prepare a quiet and private place for this exercise, making your-
    selves as comfortable as possible. Set a timer for two minutes.
    Turn toward each other and look into the eyes of your partner.
    Hold eye contact for a full two minutes. If either of you breaks
    eye contact, start the time over. You will not be speaking while
    you do this exercise. Observe and listen with your eyes, looking
    into the heart of your partner. When the timer goes off, share
    your experience with each other. You may use the following
    questions:

    *   Was this experience uncomfortable for you? Why or why
        not?

    *   What was difficult about this exercise?

    *   If eye contact is uncomfortable for you, share with your part-
        ner when this became a problem. When did you start hiding
        in this way? Why?

    *   What would be a practical way you could practice eye contact
        with each other on a daily basis? How could this be built in as
        a habit? What guidelines would you like to establish? Clarify
        your commitments to each other and communicate them
        directly. Write them down so that they will be remembered.

2. As you think about your "first healing" (your ability to know
    and experience God's love for you), answer the following
    questions:[14]

    *   How do you think God views you? What is your view of
        God?

    *   What would you like to change about your relationship with
        God?

    *   What commitments are you ready to make regarding your
        spiritual relationship with him?

    *   How can your partner support you? What specific request
        would you like to make of each other?

14. Practical resources on the love of God include Manning, *Abba's Child* and *The
Ragamuffin Gospel*; Wilson, *Into Abba's Arms*; and Yancey, *What's So Amazing about
Grace?*

3. As you think about your "second healing" (relational health and healing of past relationships), answer the following questions:

   • What did your mother teach you about yourself? Your father? How has this shaped your sense of self today?

   • Did you ever "feel felt" by your mother? How about your father? Do you "feel felt" by your spouse? Why or why not?

   • As you think about what was most damaging as well as most positive in your relationship with your parents, what one request would you like to make of your spouse regarding your need to feel emotionally connected?

   • Describe how you believe God feels about you. Why? How has this affected your relationship with him?

4. Read Psalm 139 out loud. Discuss God's truths that you observe in this passage.

5. End this time by putting your arms around each other, kneeling by the chair or bed, and praying for each other. Attune your prayers to what you have learned about each other during this exercise. Pray for protection for your relationships and strength to follow through with promises made, and make bold declarations of your love for God and each other.

Stage Three: Voice to Voice

He languished over the malaise of leaving her. How could he marry a woman he didn't know? Unraveling a riddle she whispered, "Study me."[15]

We settle for so little. When we think of the individual complexities of a man or woman, we are surprised by how little we really know about each other. Culturally, we are conditioned to "live and let live," and this has produced relational lethargy. It is rare to sit across from someone who eagerly and passionately pursues knowing us and takes the time to ask specific questions that draw us out. Sadly, this can be most poignantly true in our closest relationships. Emotional communication is the vehicle through which we experience each other; it is:

> [T]he ability and desire to put our inner world into words. It involves a commitment to live in marriage like Christ lived on this earth, "full of grace and truth" (John 1:14). We are often instructed in Scripture to speak the truth and to speak it in love. This cannot be done apart from emotional maturity and godliness.[16]

15. C. Tracy paraphrase of the movie *The Constant Gardener*.
16. Spencer and Tracy, *Marriage at the Crossroads*, 150.

In other words, emotional communication is the courageous sharing of who we really are—our naked selves.[17] While it does involve sharing negative feelings and experiences, it is not simply spouting out every negative feeling that pops into our head. The latter is what we call venting, and involves a rash and often angry self-focused disregard of the other person. When we speak of harmful negative venting, we are not addressing the meaningful sharing of deeper frustration and pain motivated by a commitment to know and be known. Such sharing of painful and difficult feelings invites others into our hidden world, whereas rash venting, which Scripture compares to a slicing sword, harms and drives others away.[18] If we entitle ourselves to the reckless venting of harsh anger in our significant relationships, we will cause deep damage.

However, we dare not overlook our angry feelings or, worse yet, deny their existence. Our anger is an important emotion to pay attention to, as it gives us valuable information about ourselves in relationship to others around us. Anger is typically a secondary emotion that serves to "defend" us from our deeper relational pain. Tracing the source of our anger will guide us to the places within our heart where hurt, fear, or sadness is buried which must be felt and expressed. We need to identify and share those deeper feelings with our spouse and closest friends so they can know us intimately. Thus, withholding our real, inner self (thoughts, feelings, and needs) as a self-protective attempt to hide from our spouse will seriously impede our intimacy.

It is important to prioritize time consistently for deeper emotional communication. This will require energy and a willingness to listen actively and enter into our partner's world. Active listening is essential, as it draws out the hidden world of another. Hence, emotional communication is a dynamic process that necessitates sensitive, interactive listening and a willingness to be vulnerably transparent with each other. Proverbs describes this well: "The purpose in a man's heart is like deep water, but a man of understanding will draw it out."[19] At first, this process can feel

---

17. Catholic ethicist James F. Keenan's unique book *Ethics of the Word*, while focused primarily on communication in the church, provides a helpful in-depth moral analysis of how believers can and should use words as the "language of love" to build trust and deepen intimacy.

18. Prov 12:18; cp. Prov 17:27–28; Eccl 10:12–14.

19. Prov 20:5 ESV. Scripture has much to say about the importance of attentive listening for understanding, loving, and responding properly to others (God and each other). For instance, see Prov 4:20; 18:13–15; 23:12; Luke 2:19; 8:18; Rev 2:7. For negative examples of this principle, see 2 Sam 13:24–29; Job 13:6; 21:2; Jer 37:14; Prov 29:19.

laborious and painfully awkward; however, with practice, it will soon become natural and life-giving. Our core thoughts and feelings must be shared so we can understand and know each other at the deepest levels.

Tim and Rhonda had been married for eight years. They came into therapy because they were having "problems" in their sex life. Although Rhonda loved her husband very much, she felt confused by how "put off" she was at the thought of having sex with him. Tim felt rejected by her negative nonverbal and verbal messages and began to quietly "shut down" emotionally and withdraw. Rhonda described Tim as the safest man she had ever known, and, therefore, felt guilty for her patterns of relational and sexual avoidance. Tim also felt guilty, particularly for the increased time he was spending away from home in pursuit of other hobbies. They were experiencing a creeping separateness that was slowly eroding the love they had consistently felt for each other from the beginning of their marriage. Tim and Rhonda wisely sought outside counsel and support, since "trying harder" was not working for them anymore. When this couple came into therapy, it was clear that they truly loved each other and wanted to stop their recursive patterns of non-intimacy. In a sense, what they most needed was structured safe and thoughtful emotional communication. I (Celestia) simply helped them put their deeper and more difficult feelings into words. I had a hunch that, if they were not articulating their pain to each other, they were also not disclosing their desire, delight, and love for each other.

I directed them first to do some personal reflection. They were to think back to their childhoods and remember five significant events that they had experienced growing up. They were to record these while they let themselves connect with the feelings of pain or pleasure they experienced at that time. Then, they were to think through the specifics of what they had needed then. This inner reflection prepared them for the next step of emotional communication.

During subsequent sessions, I guided them in sharing these memories with each other until they could understand, feel, and connect to the pain of the other. During this time of emotional communication, I required them to look each other in the eyes (this is not a furtive glance *at* the eyes and then a fixation on the floor) and to give each other focused attention (cell phones off, laps free of clutter, bodies turned toward each other, leaning forward with arms relaxed). I coached this couple toward a level of emotional intimacy they had never experienced before.

As Rhonda shared for the fist time the pain of her childhood sexual abuse and her subsequent destructive relationships in high school, I watched Tim import her pain into his soul and hold it with her. She had never told him about "her past" because she was sure he would blame and shame her in the same manner that she had done to herself. Of course, this was a terrifying process for her, yet she loved him enough to risk exposing her real self and come out of hiding. Much to her surprise and delight, as he listened, he began spontaneously to move toward her, eventually scooping her into his arms while they both wept together. He comforted her like she had never been comforted before. He felt what she felt and moved toward her in her shame and pain. I was so moved by the sacredness of this moment that I left the room to give them the privacy and time they needed for this deeper level of intimacy. She had never been that honest with him before, and, thus, they began to lay a real foundation of trust. Until she had really shared with him the events of her life that had profoundly shaped her, he couldn't know or truly love the real her. She began to understand that, when she withheld her true self, she silently abandoned him.

Conversely, Tim began to understand that, when he is emotionally dishonest and does not confront Rhonda when she hurts him by her rejection (her harsh words and demeaning tone) or abandonment, he ironically abandons her and thus fails to protect their marriage. Since the inception of their relationship, he had wanted nothing more than to be the man who loved her well and kept her safe! As he reframed his role of loving her, he began to practice a new level of emotional honesty with her also. She began to feel pursued within their relationship, and more loved. This new level of emotional honesty also made her feel more secure. She began to respect him in ways she had not in the past, because he would not let himself be put off by her anger. Neither would he own it—she was held accountable in ways that she described as "saving her from herself." I watched him learn to take the risk of letting her into his heart and admit to his own pain—to feel that pain in front of her—to cry. His emotional vulnerability moved her, and she began to feel his pain for the first time—the pain that she had caused. It was easier for her to join him in this honest and exposed place when he had gone first. She let herself feel him and move toward him as she felt his pain.

Finally, there is the healing of direct confession, repentance, and forgiveness that is quickly followed by the sweet reward of relief, joy, and closeness. The bonding that begins to grow is well worth the effort. As a couple practices this kind of emotional honesty, it becomes in time as natural and necessary as their very breath. It is their oxygen, their life essence.

In conclusion, I (Celestia) would like to share a personal example of the benefits and process of emotional intimacy. After working for more than thirty years within our marriage to build in the habits of love-driven emotional honesty, I know my husband exceedingly well. I can imagine at any moment what his thoughts, feelings, and reactions will be in a given interaction. He is in me and I am in him. I get him.

It was late afternoon Thursday as I climbed exhausted into my car after a full week of counseling. I was full of more emotion than I realized and automatically called Steve to talk. He is my favorite conversationalist, my confidant, and my closest friend. He is wise, rational, and stabilizing for my erratic heart. He is my solid place to land. When I am tired, I sometimes feel as wobbly as a top, unsteady and weary, in desperate need of centering and strength. It was one of those moments, and, before I knew what had happened, I was venting about my day. I was angry and frustrated, tired and worn out, impatient and graceless. When I stopped to catch my breath, Steve was quiet. There was a deafening silence on the phone. I immediately connected to what I had done—demolition.[20] I had dumped my pain and frustration about injustice in our world upon a man who carries that pain daily. I was able to connect quickly to *his* pain and feel the effects of my insensitivity without a laborious conversation about it, because we have had so many of those in the past! I already got it. Therefore, it was a straightforward process for me to get home, walk into his study, put my arms around his neck, and tell him I was sorry. I knew the drill. We already had established communication, and I just had to tap back into it. We were connected again and celebrated with a kiss!

Exercises and Questions for Reflection and Sharing: Voice to Voice

1.   After individually completing and scoring the Emotional Intimacy Quotient exercise in the appendices, share your results with each other. Answer the following questions:

---

20. Walter Wanger's powerful essay "Edification/Demolition" on the power of our words to build up or to tear down echoed in my ears.

- As I look at my score, am I naturally more comfortable with *knowing* or *being known*? Why is this? To what significant events in my past might this pattern be connected?

- How does this pattern play out in our relationship?

- If you could make a specific request of me regarding our emotional communication, what would it be? Why have you not asked this of me before? Or, if you have, what is standing in the way of me offering this to you?

2. Describe a time when you felt "felt" by me. How did this make you feel about yourself? How did this make you feel toward me?

3. Describe a time when you felt closest to the Lord. What Scripture did he use, or how did he communicate his love to you? How were you able to feel it? Describe the relationship you long to have with him. How can your partner support you in this? Do you need to make a specific request?

4. Create a notebook for your relationship. Divide it into four sections. Title the first section "Emotional Intimacy" and record the customized guidelines you will remember to follow in loving each other in emotional ways. What will this look like? What will you each remember to build in to your relationship as a part of your habits of love? Record these specifically. Use pictures if you like. This notebook, when completed, will be the blueprint for your "House of Love."

5. End this time by putting your arms around each other while kneeling by the chair or bed and pray for each other. Attune your prayers to what you have learned about each other in this exercise. Make bold declarations of your love for God and each other, praying for protection for your relationship and strength to follow through with promises made.

5

Relational Dimension

The Art of Cherishing

> Passion is the quickest to develop, and the quickest to fade. Intimacy develops more slowly, and commitment more gradually still.
>
> —Robert Sternberg

IT WAS FORTY YEARS ago, and I (Steve) still vividly recall the exact moment of transformation—the day and the hour I catapulted from boyhood into adolescence. My mother had taken me shopping at our local mall. After touring my favorite exotic pet store, we went to the adjacent cafeteria for lunch. As we sat down, I immediately noticed a girl my age sitting at a nearby table. In my short twelve-year life span, I had had casual friendships with many girls. There had been a few girls, particularly Sarah, my second-grade crush, who had stimulated short-lived "puppy love." But, sitting in the cafeteria that day, I experienced something qualitatively different. I looked at this petite, brown-haired girl in a different way than I had looked at any girl before. She attracted me, interested me, and stirred up unprecedented feelings inside me. I just knew she was quite captivated by my presence, as she kept glancing my way. I had never been so aware of, or more interested in, the opposite sex. Throughout my ensuing early adolescence, my interest in girls was unrequited, even though I was awkward, shy, and rarely noticed by my peers. However, during my sophomore year of high school, things began to change. I had the good fortune of making the varsity football team. The girls who had not previously given me the time of day were suddenly my "best friends." I was in hog heaven!

Following this fortuitous turn of events, I confidently began to pursue conversations with many girls. A couple of these actually evolved into deeper relationships. These relationships were intense, but shallow and short-lived. I was not bonded to any of these girls, although I had fallen "head over heels" for several of them. In hindsight, it seems I was in love with being in love. Most of us have experienced this—the ecstasy, irrationality, and evanescence of romance. Helen Fisher has conducted fascinating research on romantic love that helps explain this phenomenon. Fisher and her colleagues surveyed more than eight hundred Americans and Japanese who had recently fallen in love. The researchers found strikingly similar experiences regardless of age, ethnicity, religious affiliation, or gender. Those experiencing new romantic love most commonly evidenced the following phenomena: focused attention (infatuation), aggrandizing the beloved (love is blind), intrusive thinking (the beloved is always on your mind), emotional fire (butterflies in the stomach), and intense energy (the heart races, sleeplessness).[1] Fisher and other researchers have also discovered that this kind of initial explosive romantic love is transitory, lasting on average twelve to seventeen months.[2] Not surprisingly, she has hypothesized that there is a biological basis for these powerful romantic effects.

To test her hypothesis, Fisher and her team conducted magnetic resonance imaging (MRI) brain scans on several hundred individuals who were experiencing strong new romance. They discovered that certain portions of the brain, particularly the more "primitive" portions that control the reward circuitry, became hyperactive when the test subjects were shown a picture of their beloved. In other words, young romantic love activates the primitive, non-rational portions of the brain that stimulate arousal, pleasure, and a sense of euphoria.[3] Romantic love is particularly associated with elevated levels of dopamine, the hormone released by pleasurable, and sometimes addictive, experiences such as sex and drug use. Romantic love really does "intoxicate," but, as with literal intoxication, it eventually wears off. Interestingly, brain scans of couples who have been together for a longer period of time show considerably different elevated brain activity, particularly in parts of the brain associated with self-awareness, the assessment of others' emotions, and memo-

1. Fisher, *Why We Love*, 6–23.
2. Ibid., 72–73; Marazziti et al., "Alteration," 741–45.
3. Fisher, *Why We Love*, 69–75.

ry.[4] The implications of this brain research for intimacy are significant. Romance and passion create a sense of connection and closeness with the beloved, but, in and of themselves, they do not accurately evidence deep intimacy.

This brings me back to my early romances. During my junior year of high school, I began dating Celestia. From our very first conversation, I knew she was special—different from any other girl. I was quite smitten, really. She had many unique and beautiful qualities that I deeply admired. Yet, it was several years before I committed myself fully to her. We were quite bonded in some ways, particularly in terms of emotional intimacy forged through hundreds of hours of vulnerably deep communication. Yet, our relationship could not develop beyond its initial and limited infatuation until I was ready to commit fully to her. After a near breakup early in college, precipitated by my failure to honor the uniqueness of Celestia and our relationship, I realized that I was about to lose her. From that point on, I was in, committed to Celestia with every fiber of my being! During the next three years, I single-mindedly pursued Celestia in order to know her at the deepest levels possible, which resulted in an intensely connected bond. We were surprised to discover that, with each day, there was even more to know about the other. On December 22, 1978, we joyfully and publicly declared a lifelong commitment to God and to each other. We pledged to "forsake all others," committing to love and honor each other until death would part us. It has been more than thirty years since I voiced these consecrated promises to Celestia, and yet I have not begun to plumb the depths of knowing and loving her.

Our wedding vows created an essential foundation for our marital intimacy—a legal and sacred one-flesh covenantal commitment that served as our launch. The challenge of marital bonding is the challenge of developing relational intimacy between two people who have taken this one-flesh vow, and yet remain two distinctly separate and sometimes selfish human beings, differing in sexuality, needs, gifts, personalities, and histories. This bonding is not created overnight by romantic passion, or even in the declaration of public vows; instead, it must be tenderly cultivated, protected, and nurtured, or it will surely die.

4. Ibid., 72–73; Bartels and Zeki, "The Neural Basis of Romantic Love," 3829–34. In particular, brain scans showed more activity in the anterior cingulated cortex and the insular cortex.

What is this bonded intimacy? It is the closeness created between two people when they experience a profound sense of knowing and being known in safe, committed relationship with each other. In other words, *relational intimacy is the bond (knowing) created by valuing, prioritizing, and treating as sacred my marriage relationship and my spouse.*[5] Each of these three elements is essential for deepening intimacy within marriage.

A SACRED FOUNDATION: COVENANTAL LOVE

Celestia was special to me when I was in high school. Seeing her on campus made my heart skip a beat in a way that seeing other girls did not. I was able to share things with her I could not share with others. She was unique to me, but I had not yet given her a supreme place in my heart. *Our relationship was special, but not yet sacred.* In college, I quickly grew to see Celestia as much more than just a beautiful girl with qualities I admired and enjoyed. I began to experience her as the one and only person God had prepared for me as my life partner. I knew that God had brought us together and that she was his incredible gift to me. As the writer of Proverbs states, "House and wealth are inherited from parents, but a prudent wife is from the LORD" (19:14). We are also convinced from Scripture that marriage itself is a sacred institution ordained by God.[6] It was God who declared that it was not good for Adam to be alone. It was God who created Eve as a perfect, equal, and complementary life partner for Adam. It was God who established marriage as a lifelong one-flesh union. It was God who mercifully gifted Celestia to me as a life companion. These convictions created a dramatically different, intentional approach within me—I prioritized, protected, and honored her as I had not done before. Our relationship had taken on a sacred and set-apart quality that made it unlike any other.

Sacred means set apart for worship and service to God, and thus worthy of supreme reverence and respect. This is similar to the biblical concept of holiness. In one sense, everything in our lives is sacred, emanating from God, and is to be used to honor and glorify him. Paul states this clearly: "Whether you eat or drink, or whatever you do, do everything for the glory of God" (1 Cor 10:31). At the same time, some

---

5. Spencer and Tracy, *Marriage at the Crossroads*, 154.
6. Gen 2:18, 21–24; Matt 19:3–6; Eph 5:31–32.

things are expressly set apart by God and for God, and thus are uniquely sacred—invested with exclusive potency and given particular guidelines from God for their care and use. Their misuse, then, brings a more severe judgment, not because God is capricious or cruel, but because he is absolutely holy, awesome, and supreme. To misuse that which he has set apart for special service is to corrupt a special gift, spurn his love, and dishonor the majestic God of the universe. There are many notable examples of this in Scripture.[7]

Marriage is truly sacred. It involves a one-flesh union created by a covenant oath made to God. We see this at the end of the creation account in Genesis 2:23–24: "Then the man said, 'This at last is bone of my bones and flesh of my flesh.'... Therefore a man leaves his father and his mother and clings to his wife, and they become one flesh." When Adam declared that Eve was "bone of his bones," he was using covenant language to declare an oath to God regarding his acceptance of the exquisite divine gift of this magnificent woman. In essence, Adam was saying "I hereby invite you, God, to hold me accountable to treat this woman as my own body."[8] Covenantal language is not only used in Adam's declaration, "bone of my bones and flesh of my flesh," but also in the subsequent description of marriage as a "leaving and cleaving."[9]

It is essential, particularly in our culture, that we truly embrace the unique sacredness of marriage. In general, most Westerners still value

7. For instance, the ark of the covenant was a uniquely sacred object that reflected God's special presence and supernatural power; it was connected with unique miracles that delivered Israel (Num 7:8–9; Josh 3:3–17; 2 Chron 5:7). Hence, specific guidelines were given for the care of the ark, which some Israelites as well as pagans ignored to their own destruction (Exod 26:33–35; 30:1–10; 1 Sam 5:1–12; 2 Sam 6:6–7). Similarly, priests were set apart to lead the people in worship of Yahweh, the only true God. Very specific guidelines were given by God for worship. So, when two priests, Nadab and Abihu, chose to disobey those guidelines and offer "strange fire" in worship, fire came from the presence of God and consumed them (Lev 10:1–3). In other words, sacred gifts carry unique value, blessing, and accountability.

8. Hugenberger, *Marriage as a Covenant*, 202, cited in Davidson, *Flame of Yahweh*, 45.

9. Wenham, *Genesis 1–15*, 70. The Hebrew verb "leave" is a potent term repeatedly used of Israel forsaking Yahweh for false gods (Jer 1:16; 2:13; 5:7). "Cling" conveys strong personal attachment, such as skin clinging to flesh and bone. It is a technical term in the Hebrew Scriptures for the sacred bond between Israel and Yahweh (Deut 10:20; Josh 22:5; 2 Sam 20:31; 2 Kgs 18:6), cf. Davidson, *Flame of Yahweh*, 45. Thus, marriage is based on a binding, lifelong, sacred covenant between two people analogous to the love covenant God made with Israel (Deut 7:7–9; 29:9–25; 1 Kgs 8:23–24; Isa 55:1–5).

marriage. For example, Americans of all social, economic, and ethnic backgrounds list "having a good marriage" high on their list of social and personal ideals.[10] The vast majority of high school seniors desire to get married; 82 percent of girls and 70 percent of boys state that, for them, "having a good marriage and family life" is "extremely important."[11] Yet, at the same time, divorce rates have quadrupled since 1970, cohabitation rates rose 1,200 percent between 1960 and 2006, and the majority of teens affirm out-of-wedlock cohabitation to be a "worthy lifestyle."[12] In other words, in our culture, marriage is a desirable ideal, but not a sacred institution. *It is special, but not sacred.* To compound this weakening of the inviolability of marriage is the fact that we live in an increasingly narcissistic and egocentric culture. The quality and value of relationships in general, and marriage in particular, are measured by what we experience in the moment—are we happy and fulfilled?[13]

Our commitment to the romantic concept of marriage will inevitably be tried and tested when we are confronted with the day-to-day realities of married life. After the honeymoon, we quickly discover that this amazing person, whom we expected to give us continual joy and bliss, to love, understand, and attentively meet our every need, has a surprising capacity to confuse, frustrate, and sometimes hurt us. It is in these moments that a deep commitment to the sacred nature of marriage is particularly vital, for it shifts and lifts our focus off subjective feelings and enlarges our vision to God's character so that we may unselfishly serve the needs of our spouse. Romance is a beautiful thing and has its place in marriage; however, it is woefully inadequate as the currency of love. We need an anchor and paradigm larger than our incomplete and restricted emotional selves. As one astute husband notes, "Romantic love has no elasticity to it. It can never be stretched; it simply shatters. Mature love, the kind demanded of a good marriage, must stretch, as the sinful human condition is such that all of us bear conflicting emotions. . . . A wedding calls us to our highest and best—in fact, to almost impossible— ideals. It's the way we want to live."[14] Understanding and committing ourselves to the sacred nature of marriage helps us live out the ideal that

10. Waite and Gallagher, *The Case for Marriage,* 174.

11. Popenoe and Whitehead, "The State of Our Unions," 26.

12. Ibid., 27.

13. See Twenge and Campbell, *The Narcissism Epidemic,* 211–29.

14. Thomas, *Sacred Marriage,* 15–16.

our hearts long for by taking us beyond our emotion and connecting us to the very heart of God.

Our commitment to the sacred, covenantal nature of marriage has made *the* difference in our thirty-two years of marriage. For instance, as newlyweds, we had several nights where we never made it to bed. Why? We were resolving conflict. We knew we did not have a relational "out," and thus were committed to understanding each other and to a complete resolution of hurt.[15] God gave us to each other, and we never looked back (or out). We made sacred vows to God and each other. For us, it was a matter of integrity. We knew that, no matter how difficult the immediate relational situation, God would give us the wisdom, grace, and strength to deal with the challenges as we looked to him.[16] Our marriage does not rise or fall on how we feel in a given moment of weakness, but on what God in his perfection and goodness declares about marriage and about us, his married children.

Not only is marriage sacred, but so is our spouse, including all of his or her natural qualities—strengths and weaknesses. Scripture teaches that God lovingly and uniquely forms us while in our mothers' wombs with the specific attributes that will allow us to carry out his unique purposes in our lives.[17] The sacred providence of God in our spouse's natural talents and traits has acute ramifications for marriage. This is especially true for habits that may seem to be natural weaknesses or even deficits. Thus, the package of gifts and qualities I appreciate in Celestia, combined with the ones that require more patience, are providentially crafted by God for my sanctification and his glory. Over the years, this concept

---

15. We actually do not recommend this strategy today, as often there are times when it is necessary to impose a "time out" to pray, cool down, and then come back together with a prepared and humble heart. However, this example from our early years of marriage illustrates the importance of perseverance toward resolution and an active relational commitment toward resolution.

16. This statement should not be construed as an idealization of marriage that does not allow for divorce under any circumstances. Marriage is ordained by God to be a permanent, lifelong union, yet God in his grace and mercy makes provision for sinful human failure. We believe Scripture allows for divorce in cases of unrepentant sexual infidelity (Matt 19:3–9), desertion (1 Cor 7:12–15), and abuse (Exod 21:10–11). It is our sacred view of marriage, and of life itself, that causes us to accept divorce as morally acceptable and even necessary in certain situations. See especially Gaither, *Redemptive Divorce;* Instone-Brewer, *Divorce and Remarriage in the Bible;* and Roberts, *Not Under Bondage.*

17. Exod 3:10–12; 4:10–14; Ps 139:13–16; Eccl 11:5; Jer 1:5.

has taken on even greater significance for us. Celestia and I committed early in our relationship intentionally to appreciate and respect the very different (and sometimes quirky) characteristics of each other. We specifically decided to guard against contempt that could breed in the soil of daily familiarity. We would work to not take each other for granted. Instead, we would consciously appreciate and nurture the unique qualities that began to emerge in each other. We would see these differences as divinely given and, therefore, reflective of the sacred ways in which we image God through our "oneness." The longer we are married, the more apparent this is for us. Today, our greatest strengths in life and ministry are the individual differences that balance and complement the other. Therefore, we have chosen never to show contempt for these dramatically different characteristics in each other privately or publicly, but, instead, to love and cherish these very differences God has ordained for us.

Our first real trial occurred during our fourth year of marriage as I was finishing my final year of seminary. Celestia had a sudden, severe accident requiring four extensive orthopedic surgeries and lengthy hospitalizations during the ensuing eighteen months. Our first child was just a baby. Needless to say, our world turned upside down and has never been quite the same. Since her original accident, Celestia has endured seventeen major surgeries. Recently, after a week of extensive testing at Mayo Clinic, we learned that she has a rare, currently incurable, degenerative disorder. This has helped us to understand her medical history better. Despite this reality, Celestia is one of the most active, productive people I know, which is one of the many things I love and admire about her. Yet, her disorder has dramatically altered our lives and limited many of our options. As an example, I have always loved intense athletic competition and physical challenge. Today, we can no longer do many of the activities we enjoyed when we were first married. Celestia's frequent surgeries have greatly impacted our schedule, our margin, and our resources. Looking at this from a purely human perspective, it might seem that her disorder is a depressing misfortune that would have dramatically discouraged both of us. In reality, nothing could be further from the truth!

Celestia's physical challenges were ordained by God for good purposes. They have deepened our relational intimacy as powerfully as anything else in our lives. As I look back on our marriage, I can now see that I was much more independent and self-focused in those early years than

I realized. When I suddenly found myself with a dependent infant and a wife in the hospital, I was forced to shift my focus. I learned to serve my family in revolutionary new ways. Celestia also found herself in a very powerless place and was forced to depend upon me in unprecedented ways. There were stretches of time when she was completely dependent upon me for her every physical need. These needs were often pressing, and I was compelled to put them above my own. Her illness has been one of my greatest gifts, for it has taught me how to love.

Our very intimacy model was birthed during these early years of pain. I experience great joy in being the one who is chosen by God to serve her in the most practical ways. Celestia's surgeries gave us countless, deeply personal experiences that have connected us more tightly to each other and to Christ. Furthermore, God used them to direct our joint ministry to others who have known great pain. Today, our great joy is that, together, we are privileged to research, write, speak, direct a non-profit organization, and to minister to leaders domestically and internationally in areas of sexuality and abuse/trauma. Our deepest satisfaction and intimacy come from our joint work. We also know that much of what we teach and write comes out of the lessons we have learned together. Pain taught us how to love each other, how to prioritize the needs of each other over our own self-interests and pleasure. We have found depths of joy and love we never dreamed possible, through sacrifice. When I see Celestia's scars, I am reminded again of how much I love her and admire the courageous and godly way she deals with daily pain. Celestia is sacred to me, as are her scars. They have been graciously ordained by God for his purposes in our lives. I am a better man for loving her.

For singles, during this relational phase of bonding, the emphasis is on a deepening friendship—the disclosure of our honest selves. Do we have shared values, and are we moving in the same direction? Without this deeper, honest sharing, a couple will move too quickly into sexual touch as a means of experiencing closeness with each other. For example, kissing beyond the conventional kiss of hello or goodbye moves a couple too quickly past this stage of bonding and into the sexual. Therefore, the wise couple restrains from sexual touch so that this early bonding can take place. The questions for reflection and discussion at the end of each stage can be utilized by both singles in an intentional relationship and by married couples. They will serve as a guide for intentional conversation that will support you in creating and deepening your relational bond.

The more you learn this self-control, the greater will become your ability to love with your heart. You will learn to recognize the kind of love that is aroused by a smile or a gesture or a certain tone of voice and which reveals the heart of a girl. This is very soft music and you need practice in order to hear it. The more you tone down the drums, the more you will become aware of it.[18]

---

18. Trobisch, *I Loved A Girl*, 15.

Stage Four: Hand to Hand

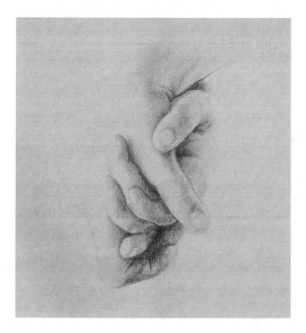

SACRED VALUE

Notice in the picture that the only physical contact is the four square inches of skin on the fingers and hands. The emphasis at this stage is on the relationship—the friendship and public statement that says, "We are now a couple." We are no longer just thinking about ourselves, but have begun the process of considering and valuing this other person whom we have chosen to pursue in relationship.

Believers are called to love, honor, and treat all people respectfully, including enemies, because all humans are made in God's image and loved by God.[19] How much more should we value our covenant spouse, not just made in God's image like all other humans, but uniquely appointed by God to be our beloved spouse. Thus, the Scriptures give poignant commands to husbands and wives about how they are to treat each other. Peter commands husbands to give their wives honor and reverence (respect) due to intrinsic value "as a fellow heir of the grace of God lest your prayers be hindered" (1 Pet 3:7). In other words, God man-

19. Matt 5:43–45; Col 3:12–13; 1 Pet 2:17; Jas 3:9–10.

dates husbands to cherish and love their wives—and threatens to ignore
the prayers of husbands who don't. Paul also commands husbands to
love, nurture, and care for their wives tenderly as they would value and
care for their own physical bodies. These unprecedented commands are
given to husbands, and not to their wives.

Wives, in turn, are told to respect their husbands (Eph 5:28–33).
The Greek word used here for "respect" is a strong term that often indicates fear or reverence. Here, it means a deep respect based on the value
of the unique marital relationship.[20] Valuing means letting our actions
and attitudes come in line with the sacred nature of marriage. If God
gave us our spouse, and he or she is our life partner by covenant, then
our spouse is of supreme value. Husbands and wives are to treat each
other as the precious gifts they actually are. Unfortunately, it is all too
easy to lose sight of this wondrous reality in the daily grind of marriage.
Often, we don't give our spouse the same value or kindness we would
give strangers. Marriage expert John Gottman argues that, as soon as
two people marry, often one of the first things lost in their interactions
is politeness.[21] He explains that this may simply be the natural result
of increasing comfort with each other; however, loss of kindness can
launch a dangerous trajectory toward disrespect, which leads to rude-
ness, which in turn leads to increased negativity toward each other.
Given the fact that, in the marriage ecosystem, negativity is the primary
"predator" threatening the relationship, marital politeness is not a minor
social courtesy; it is essential. Thus, seemingly trivial acts of respect or
disrespect are ultimately quite significant in developing the sacred value
of our marriages.

There are several practical ways in which we can value our spouses.

Mutual Sacrifice

Love is developed through self-sacrifice. The nature of leaving, cleaving,
and becoming one flesh embeds sacrifice into the very fabric of married
life. Marriage vows create a radically new one-flesh reality that super-

20. *Phobeomai.* This verb is used to indicate having fear in the sense of great reverence (Luke 1:50; Acts 10:35; Col 3:22) and of respect for humans "who command
respect" (Lev 19:3; Eph 5:33). Danker, ed., *A Greek-English Lexicon,* 1061–62. In the
context of Eph 5:33, it seems the husband "commands respect" by virtue of the marriage
relationship.

21. Gottman, *Why Marriages Succeed or Fail,* 65–66.

sedes the husband's and wife's previous existence as singles. Even when one is engaged or cohabiting, the security and finality of the relational bond is not the same as in marriage. It is much easier to exit the relationship if things get rough. Furthermore, unmarried couples still have their own individual existence; not all of life is shared. In a very real sense, "two becoming one" brings death as surely as it brings new life. The day we were married, we no longer had our own separate surnames, possessions, living spaces, or bank accounts. It was no longer "mine" and "yours," but "ours." In large and small ways, we learned to sacrifice for the primacy and health of our marriage. If we truly believe that our spouse is given to us as a precious gift by our loving heavenly Father, then sacrificing for our marriage will be a privilege and not a burden. The Old Testament story of Jacob and Rachel portrays this sacrifice. For instance, in order to be able to marry Rachel, Jacob labored for her father Laban seven years, but "they seemed to him but a few days because of the love he had for her" (Gen 29:20). Of course, some necessary marital sacrifices are painful and difficult, but, if we truly love our spouse and love the God who gave him or her to us, then sacrificing for our covenant lover will bring more joy than anguish.

God calls husbands and wives to mutual, though not identical, sacrifice. Ephesians 5:21 commands husbands and wives to "be subject [submit] to one another out of reverence for Christ."[22] To "be subject" means to sacrifice voluntarily for each other, to set aside our own interests and yield to the needs of our spouse. A few of these differing sacrifices are obvious and fixed. For instance, the woman uniquely sacrifices her body to bear a child, the physical fruit of a couple's love and sexual intimacy. Due to biological gender differences, particularly greater levels of testosterone, men are most often physically stronger than women. Therefore, in some contexts, husbands will make unique physical sacrifices to care for and protect their wives. Paul's commands to wives and husbands later on in Ephesians 5 are not identical. For instance, he targets husbands with the command to nurture and care for their wives sacrificially as they would their own bodies. Many, if not most, of our differing sacri-

---

22. We should note that, while virtually all egalitarians interpret Eph 5:21 as a call to mutual submission, this is not exclusively an egalitarian reading of this verse. For instance, see Lincoln, *Ephesians*, 366. This reading best accounts for language of the passage and is very similar to other, less-disputed "mutual deference" commands given by Paul (Gal 5:13; Eph 4:2; Phil 2:3–4).

fices stem from our differing personalities and needs. Regardless of the
specifics, the point is that husbands and wives are mutually to sacrifice
for each other, and in doing so they will increasingly deepen their relational bond.

One of the most powerful and beautiful examples of joyful sacrifice for one's partner as a reflection of the sacredness of marriage comes
from J. Robertson McQuilkin. Dr. McQuilkin was a highly respected
author, speaker, and president of Columbia International University.
In the prime of his career, Muriel, his wife of more than four decades,
was diagnosed with Alzheimer's disease. A few years later, as her health
declined, he resigned his presidency to stay at home and care for her full
time. He described his decision to leave his college ministry in terms of
his love for Muriel and the sacred nature of his marriage vows in a 1990
article:

> When the time came, the decision was firm. It took no great
> calculation. It was a matter of integrity. Had I not promised,
> 42 years before, "in sickness and in health . . . till death do us
> part"? . . . This was no grim duty to which I was stoically re-
> signed, however. It was only fair. She had, after all, cared for
> me for almost four decades with marvelous devotion; now it
> was my turn. And such a partner she was! If I took care of her
> for 40 years, I would never be out of her debt. . . . It is all more
> than keeping promises and being fair, however. As I watch her
> brave descent into oblivion, Muriel is the joy of my life. Daily I
> discern new manifestations of the kind of person she is, the wife
> I always loved. I also see fresh manifestations of God's love—the
> God I long to love more fully.[23]

Six years later, as Muriel had declined to the point that she could no
longer talk, McQuilkin wrote another article. He states:

> Seventeen summers ago, Muriel and I began our journey into the
> twilight. It's midnight now, at least for her, and sometimes I won-
> der when dawn will break. Even the dread Alzheimer's disease
> isn't supposed to attack so early and torment so long. Yet, in her
> silent world, Muriel is so content, so loveable. If Jesus took her
> home, how I would miss her gentle, sweet presence. . . . Valentine's
> Day was always special in our house because that was the day
> in 1948 Muriel accepted my marriage proposal. On the eve of
> Valentine's day in 1995 I read a statement by some specialist that

---

23. McQuilkin, "Living by Vows," 38–40.

Alzheimer's is the most cruel disease of all, but that the victim is actually the caregiver. I wondered why I never felt like a victim. That night I entered in my journal: "The reason I don't feel like a victim is—I'm not!" When others urged me to call it quits, I responded, "Do you realize how lonely I would be without her?"[24]

McQuilkin lovingly cared for his wife for thirteen years after he left Columbia. She died in 2003. He did not consider it a sacrifice to give up his presidency in order to serve her. For him, marriage and Muriel were sacred.

Mutual Respect

In the first year of our marriage, we looked around at the state of marriages in our society and decided that there would have to be intentional commitments made to build and then protect the love between us, that there was no way our love would accidently grow strong and enduring. Therefore, we set about the task of commitments—specific and sure—to build a castle for our love. It was easiest for us to begin with the things we would not do or did not want to do as a part of our marriage:

1. We would not allow "creeping separateness"[25] to silently erode our "in-loveness." Therefore, everything would be shared. If one of us enjoyed a thing, the other would learn to enjoy it. We would look for the beauty in the activity or the preference enjoyed by the other until it was personally enjoyed by us both. We would not be a couple who lived increasingly separate lives. Each year, we would move more intentionally toward the other, not away. Each year we would experience more depth, more love, more sharing.

2. We would build a foundation of total trust. All things would be communicated and shared. We would create daily time for unpressured communication and sharing. We would not keep secrets from each other or fail to share significant events or thoughts of our days. "Our trust in each other would not just be based on love and loyalty but on the fact of a thousand sharings—a thousand strands twisted into something unbreakable."[26]

24. McQuilkin, "Muriel's Blessing," 32–34.
25. Vanauken, *A Severe Mercy*, 27.
26. Ibid.

3. We would mutually value and develop the abilities and interests of the other. One set of dreams or goals would not be sacrificed for the other. We would mutually sacrifice for each other. As an example, I joyfully taught school so that Steve could complete his seminary education, and he then sacrificially worked a second job so I could complete my master's degree in psychology. We saw these as opportunities to serve each other and to invest in God's purposes for us as individuals and as a couple.

4. We would resolve all conflict before going to bed. We would seek to stay close and engaged with each other no matter how difficult—to embrace the frustration and hurt in the offended, until we could again experience the love. We would learn to listen until we understood the offended before launching our own proud defense. We would allow our love for God and each other to produce a humble posture of repentance and forgiveness in each of us. We would stay engaged with each other until mutual resolution was reached. This would make a way for understanding each other in new ways that would alter our future interactions. We would practice daily humble acts of forgiveness that would protect and enhance our love.

5. We would pray together every day, anchoring our love and promises to each other in God's love for us, and our desire to please him.

Mutual Affirmation

The practice of mutual affirmation involves both praising your spouse directly and praising him or her to others. Our spouse and closest friends need to hear us regularly affirm and praise each other, including their God-given physical features, talents, gifts, character, and unique traits of personality. There are numerous beautiful biblical examples of effusive praise for one's spouse and intimate friends. The Apostle Paul gave specific affirmation to his readers in the first portion of all but one of his thirteen letters. He was bold in stating how much he loved, appreciated, and missed his friends. For example, he told the Philippians, "For God is my witness, how I long for you all with the affection of Christ Jesus. . . . [M]y beloved brethren whom I long to see, my joy and crown" (Phil 1:8; 4:1).

Our affirmation must include our appreciation of our spouse's physical qualities as well as inner beauty. Song of Solomon gives poetic examples of effusive praise of both outer beauty and inner character. Note the detailed praise this woman offers her beloved:

> What is your beloved more than another beloved, O fairest among women? What is your beloved more than another beloved, that you thus adjure us? My beloved is all radiant and ruddy, distinguished among ten thousand. His head is the finest gold; his locks are wavy, black as a raven. His eyes are like doves beside springs of water, bathed in milk, fitly set. His cheeks are like beds of spices, yielding fragrance. His lips are lilies, distilling liquid myrrh. His arms are rounded gold, set with jewels. His body is ivory work, encrusted with sapphires. His legs are alabaster columns, set upon bases of gold. His appearance is like Lebanon, choice as the cedars. His speech is most sweet, and he is altogether desirable. This is my beloved and this is my friend, O daughters of Jerusalem.
>
> —Song 5:9—6:1

Is this kind of affirmation a habit within your intimate relationship? We live in an increasingly caustic, critical, and sarcastic time. Words of specific affirmation are critical to our ongoing love and well-being. Commit to absolute loyalty and kindness that increases with the years. Publicly and privately thank your spouse for the unique traits and strengths he or she brings into the marriage. Express your delight! This is essential to honoring each other. Often, when I (Celestia) am at our seminary, Steve's students will come up to me and comment on the love he has expressed for me in his classes. This greatly deepens my sense of value and security in our relationship. It is also a beautiful echo of the love that Christ has for us, his bride.

Exercises and Questions for Reflection and Sharing: Hand to Hand—Sacred Value

1. Do you remember your mother respecting or disrespecting your father? What were ways you absorbed her disrespect of him? How was her respect/disrespect communicated within their marriage? What was the effect upon you—then and now?

2. How did your father communicate his respect for your mom? His disrespect? How do you think you were affected by him and his patterns of relating to your mom? How might your father's pattern

of respect or disrespect be impacting you within your significant relationships today?

3. Our deepest intimacy needs within our significant relationships are typically connected to our unmet needs as children. The key to a customized "designer love" which results in relational bondedness is to understand the relational pain your partner has experienced and then to customize your habits of loving to his or her specific and felt relational needs.

4. Ask your partner to share how he or she feels most respected in relationship with you. ("I feel most respected by you when you _____.")

5. Ask how she or he felt disrespected. Listen quietly without making excuses or defending yourself. Remember, your goal is to understand your beloved in ways you have not before so that you can love more intimately. Now make specific requests of each other. ("I would feel more respected by you if you would _____.")

6. Express your specific gratitude to each other. ("Thank you for _____.")

7. Together, read Proverbs 31:10–12, 26–30, and share with each other what application you feel compelled to make from this text. Are there any confessions you need to make to each other? If so, do it now.

8. Are there any specific guidelines you want to build into your relationship? If so, write them down and keep them in a place where you will see them every day as a couple.

9. Pray a blessing over each other. Build the habit of prayer into each evening, before going to bed.

Stage Five: Arm to Shoulder

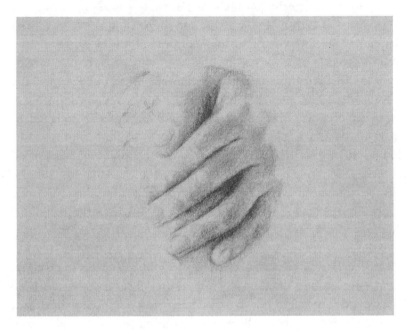

SACRED PRIORITY

What is the progression you notice in this picture? This couple has increased their private and public intention of being "one"—not two singles, but one couple. This progression requires more sacrifice, less independence, and more personal responsibility taken for the relationship.

"Therefore a man leaves his father and his mother and clings to his wife" (Gen 2:24) is a commonly cited passage, particularly at weddings. However, the shocking thrust of this verse easily evades us in its English translation. The Hebrew verb translated "leave" is a forceful term which, in this context, is best translated as "abandon" or "forsake." This word is frequently used in the Old Testament to describe Israel forsaking Yahweh for false gods.[27] A literal reading of this verse would have sounded shocking and utterly unacceptable to ancient Jews who placed great value on honoring one's parents and extended family. Furthermore, ancient Jewish culture was patrilocal; that is, the husband stayed near his family and the family land that he would someday inherit. The wife left

---

27. Deut 28:20; Jer 1:16; 2:13; 5:7; 16:11. The Hebrew verb is 'ázob.

her family to come live with her new husband and his extended family.[28]
So, in this Genesis account, Moses isn't speaking of a man literally aban-
doning his family to cling to his wife. Rather, this is jolting metaphorical language to convey the dramatic and thorough manner in which a
man must make his wife the absolute priority of his life above all other
loyalties. To prioritize your wife above your parents is to make her the
"top tier." This is similar to Jesus' shocking statement in Luke 14:26 that
to be his disciple one must hate parents, spouse, children, and siblings.
Jesus was certainly not commanding his followers literally to hate family members, which would violate many other biblical commands, including the fifth of the Ten Commandments, "Honor your father and
mother." This jolting metaphorical language indicates that love for God
must be supreme above all earthly loyalties and relationships, including
family. Similarly, then, in marriage, we must prioritize marriage above all
other relationships.

The covenant language used repeatedly in Genesis 2:24–25 reminds
us that marriage involves a sacred priority and, as such, is to be all encompassing. It must dramatically impact literally every aspect of life—
how we spend our time, how we spend and view our money, the dreams
and hobbies we pursue, etc. Every decision is made and filtered through
love—what will be best for our relationship? Should one give up a particular hobby or the other learn to participate in it? What decision would
prioritize our relationship and protect it for a lifetime of love? Each must
be ready to sacrifice for the sake of the other and the relationship.

For young Israelite newlyweds, God mandated a unique prioritization in the first year of marriage. Moses commanded, "[W]hen a man
takes a new wife, he shall not go out with the army, nor be charged with
any duty; he shall be free at home one year and shall give happiness
to his wife whom he has taken" (Deut 24:5 NASB). Several things are
noteworthy about this text. First of all, it comes immediately after instructions regarding divorce. Divorce was a concession granted by God
due to the reality of human sinfulness, but it was not part of his beautiful
plan for human relationships. If Jewish couples, particularly husbands,
carefully obeyed the brief instructions in Deuteronomy 24:5, the divorce
instructions in the preceding four verses would be utterly unnecessary.
It should also be noted that, while Deuteronomy 24:5 is brief, it is all

28. Wenham, "Family in the Pentateuch," 17–18. For biblical examples, see Gen
24:1–66 and 30:26 (Rebekah, Rachel, and Leah).

encompassing. Husbands were essentially to drop all their normal duties and activities to prioritize learning to love and nurture their wives. This might also suggest that women are a bit complex and there is a learning curve involved in learning to meet their needs; creating a foundation of love takes time—lots of it.

Obviously, in our modern cultures, few newly married couples can suspend their normal responsibilities for the first year of marriage. Yet, this passage is more culturally relevant that it might appear. Research on American young married couples shows that the number-one marital frustration is lack of time together due to the demands of work.[29] We simply cannot have it all and do it all. Couples can and must find radical ways to prioritize each other by sacrificing other, lesser priorities. This certainly includes being willing to live more simply so they do not need to work as many hours.

Willard Harley, a Christian psychologist, conducted some interesting research with Christian married couples that is summarized in his book, *His Needs, Her Needs*. He found that happily married couples needed a minimum of fifteen hours per week to maintain an already intimate marriage.[30] This is time spent in focused interactive activities as a couple. These fifteen hours would not include time spent watching television or movies, or in activities with other couples or children. We have found this figure to be a true guide in our marriage. Clearly, this time will not automatically appear and must be intentionally inserted into each day of the week so that it will be unhurried, unpressured, and relaxed.

Exercises and Questions for Reflection and Sharing:
Arm to Shoulder—Sacred Priority

1. Reflect on your childhood memories again. What were the priorities in your childhood home? How were these communicated? How did your parents' family/marriage priorities impact you as a child? As an adolescent? Take time to share this with each other.

2. If you had owned a magic wand as a child, what would you have changed growing up? Why? What difference might this have made?

29. Schramm et al., "After 'I Do.'"
30. Harley, *His Needs, Her Needs*, 58–59.

3. On a scale of one to ten, pick a number that best fits your attempts to prioritize your partner and his or her relational needs. List the ways in which you intentionally prioritize them.

4. On a scale of one to ten, pick a number that best fits your experience of being prioritized by your partner. In other words, if you feel prioritized 100 percent of the time, you would pick the number ten. If not at all, you would pick the number one. List the ways in which you feel prioritized. List the ways in which you do not.

5. When you are both done with your lists, gently share them with each other. This exercise will give you practice at direct, but respectful, emotional communication.

6. Keep short accounts with each other. If there are behaviors you need to confess and change, do so now. Breathe the *oxygen* of healthy relationships—confession and forgiveness. ("I realize that I have _____ in our relationship. I now understand that these choices have hurt you in the following ways: _____. I regret hurting you and want to confess to you my sin of _____. I will demonstrate my heart of repentance by taking the following steps: _____. Thank you for giving me grace and the opportunity to change.")

7. "I want to say 'thank you' for _____."

8. "Our plan for creating the margin of fifteen hours per week for focused interactive time for our relationship is _____."

9. End this time in prayer. Kneel together and take each other's hand. You cannot make changes in your marriage by your own strength. Ask for God's help and guidance as you purpose to follow through with the commitments you have made to each other.

Stage Six: Arm to Waist

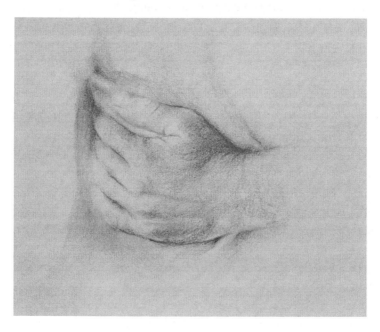

SACRED PROTECTION

The couple is not face to face yet, but their bodies are pulled close together in a more intimate embrace. They are not yet lovers, but more than friends. For singles, it is important that this stage not be rushed. There is much to determine at this point before you commit and give yourself more fully to each other. Will my partner protect and prioritize our relationship? Is he trustworthy? Does he prioritize his relationship with Christ? Is she committed to following the teachings of Scripture? Does she communicate vulnerable information about herself? Can she trust me with the truth about her past? Does he demonstrate the capacity and desire to give of his time unselfishly in order to truly know me, without receiving anything sexual from our relationship? Does she have an interest in me, or does she just want to be in a relationship because of a fear of being alone? Do I feel valued and cherished by him? Does he respect my very different relational needs? Do we want the same things relationally? Are we really going in the same life direction? "It is during this sixth step, arm to waist, that enough of the life visions of each are disclosed that a decision about the future of the relationship is urgent. This is the 'last exit' on the pair-bonding freeway."[31]

Now, we will turn our attention to married couples. On March 30, 1981, John Hinckley, Jr., shot President Ronald Reagan outside the Washington Hilton Hotel. I (Steve) will never forget the newspaper photos the next day of Secret Service agents throwing themselves in front of the president, using their bodies as a costly shield. I am confident that these agents did not risk their lives simply because they were loyal Republicans, but because they had taken a solemn oath and took their commitment seriously. In 2009, the United States spent $25 million to protect its former presidents and their families, and millions more protecting President Barack Obama. Even though every American citizen has equal constitutional rights and is to be given freedom and justice, there is only one president. He (or, someday, possibly she) holds the highest political office in the land and, because of the uniqueness of this office, no expense is spared in protecting this person. Similarly, if we truly believe that marriage is sacred and precious, we will protect our marriage at all costs.

Scripture gives many examples and injunctions regarding marital protection. For instance, in Proverbs, Solomon repeatedly admonishes his son to guard against threats to his marriage. He specifically instructs him to take concrete protective measures to guard his marriage against emotional and sexual affairs.[32] Some of these include keeping far away from the house of immoral women, pursuing wisdom at all costs, rejoicing in your wife, cultivating sexual intimacy with your wife, guarding your heart, avoiding the flattering glances of immoral women, not allowing your heart to desire the beauty of another woman, and carefully watching the life decisions you make.

When I think of "hand to waist" protection, I think of our travel to unfamiliar places and countries. I am flooded with memories of Steve firmly placing his arm securely aroung my waist and tucking me in close. This is not only a nonverbal signal that I am with him and that he is protecting me, but also a metaphor for other kinds of relational protection. Some of the steps we have taken to protect our relationship include establishing written, mutually agreed-upon guidelines; establishing a network of wise counselors/friends who know us intimately—including

31. Joy, *Bonding*, 47.
32. Prov 2:16–22; 5:3–20; 6:20–35; 7:5–25; 22:14.

our inner struggles, insecurities, and weaknesses—and mentors whom we have invited to speak wisdom into our lives; committing to a minimum of fifteen hours per week of focused time with each other; and painstakingly cultivating our spiritual lives through spiritual retreats, regular journaling, fasting, and prayer.

In our cultural context, it is particularly important that husbands and wives zealously protect each other against sexual sin. Sexual intimacy is an incredibly powerful and beautiful expression of a one-flesh relationship. It also serves to deepen oneness. Men and women are both sexual beings equally capable of sexual fulfillment as well as sexual sin. Hence, both must protect their marriage by pursuing sexual healing (where that is needed) so they can enjoy a mutually satisfying sexual relationship. We must also guard against the temptation to meet our sexual and emotional needs apart from our spouse, because God has exclusively ordained our spouse to meet these needs and to support us. Hence, we steal from our spouse and undermine the very foundation of marriage when we meet our sexual and emotional needs apart from each other. Primarily due to the fact that men have, on average, ten to twenty times more testosterone than women, and women generally have much higher levels of estrogen, males tend to have higher libido and have a greater tendency to divorce the sex act from the relationship. This makes husbands more susceptible to meeting their powerful sexual needs through pornography. Sadly, when a husband sexually satiates himself by looking at porn and masturbating, he breaks his relational intimacy with his wife by dissipating his sexual energy apart from her. He also experiences shame and guilt, which creates a desire to hide. When a husband guards his sexual purity and commits himself to meet his sexual needs only with his wife, it will create great passion and movement toward her, which reinforces relational intimacy. Some of the specific steps we have taken to protect our marriage sexually include my (Steve's) subscription to Internet blocking and tracking software, sharing our cell phone and computer passwords with each other, prioritizing our sexual relationship, and communicating honestly to each other any ongoing sexual attraction from or toward another person.

In many respects, it is easiest to view marriage as sacred in the early days of a relationship when romantic passion is fresh and intense. The challenge is to retain that perspective and love for each other over the course of time as we become familiar with our partner's quirks and idiosyncrasies. If we do not, our love may cool and erode that special sense of God's providence in bringing us together for his purposes and eternal plan. Likewise, our covenant love relationship with our heavenly Father can become mundane and stale over time. For example, this is exactly what happened to the church in Ephesus, prompting God to warn, "I have this against you, that you have left your first love" (Rev 2:4).

We suggest reflecting consciously on the story of your relationship, particularly when you are frustrated with your spouse, reminding yourself of the providential goodness of God reflected in your unique relational history. Such a reframe will powerfully clarify and correct wrong perceptions as you reflect on what drew you and your spouse together, what you found attractive about him or her, and how God has worked in your relationship. This story is a part of your narrative: an oral history spoken again and again as you celebrate God's hand upon you![33]

Exercises and Questions for Reflection and Sharing:
Arm to Waist—Sacred Protection

1. Did you feel protected growing up? Describe.

2. When were you not protected as a child? How has this impacted you? What are your specific relational needs today as a result of your experiences as a child?

3. Do you feel secure in your marriage (or dating) relationship? Why or why not?

4. Reflect back on your relational history, including your childhood. Describe the time(s) you have felt the safest. What was done or not done, said or not said, that created this safe relationship?

---

33. This is somewhat similar to what the secular marriage researcher John Gottman describes. Gottman is arguably the leading marriage researcher in America. He finds a couple's view of their relational history to be particularly telling. In fact, couples' written answers regarding their history allowed Gottman to predict with 94 percent accuracy which couples would divorce. He states that "nothing foretells a marriage's future as accurately as how a couple retells their past." He goes on to note that, when a marriage is unraveling, the couple begins to "recast their earlier times in a negative light." (*Why Marriages Succeed or Fail,* 127). In this same book, Gottman gives some excellent practical exercises to help couples "glory in their marital story" (224–28).

5. Tell your partner the ways you feel most protected by him/her. How has this made you feel? How has this impacted the ways in which you respond to him/her?

6. What would you like to change in your relationship? What do you want to remain the same?

7. What could your partner offer you that would help you feel safer and more protected? Explain your answers to each other and then make a specific request(s) of each other.

8. End this time with prayer, praying for the specific needs of each other and the relationship. Thank God for his blessings and provision in your life. Ask for his guidance as you learn to trust his principles and live them out in your relationship.

6

Physical Dimension

The Power of Touch

> Our bodies have eighteen square feet of skin, which makes skin our largest organ. Because skin cannot shut its eyes or cover its ears, it is on a constant state of readiness to receive messages—it is always on. The first sensory input in life comes from the sense of touch while still in the womb, and touch continues to be the primary means of experiencing the world throughout infancy and well into childhood, even into aging.
>
> —Tiffany Field[1]

O NE OF THE MOST important, and often neglected, aspects of bonding is nonerotic, affectionate touch. Just as a baby is born essentially "unattached" and is completely dependent upon the mother (and other caregivers) for its very survival, so are we dependent upon each other for our relational health and wellbeing. Just as the infant receives a multisensory "bath" of rocking, cooing, feeding, and smiling that transforms the brain and develops and enhances the capacity for emotional and relational intimacy later in life, so are we dependent upon each other for healthy touch to develop and enhance our relational and personal lives. In a sense, the more we touch, the more we want to touch and be touched.

Before we address the practical applications of touch, let's begin by understanding the cultural context in which we live and build relationships.

1. Field, *Touch,* 10.

OUR CULTURAL LANDSCAPE:
LAND OF THE TOUCH-STARVED

By world standards, Westerners appear to lack very little. For example, we enjoy one of the highest standards of living in the history of civilization. Our literacy and education rate is robust, advanced technology is ubiquitous, and material blessings abound. Given the fact that the U.S. Centers for Disease Control and Prevention estimates two-thirds of American adults to be either overweight or obese, one could easily conclude that we have too much, not too little. Yet, when it comes to one of the most essential commodities in life, nonerotic affectionate touch, we are some of the most impoverished people in the world.

It wasn't until our family began traveling internationally and were surprised to see men walking down the street arm in arm in Turkey and Uganda; men and women comfortably touching strangers on the arms, shoulders, and back in Italy (which felt like an invasion of personal space to us); and Congolese mothers and girls spending the entire day with sleepy, relaxed babies strapped securely to their backs that we began to realize how much less we Americans touch than do people of other cultures. We vividly remember our daughter Abby's first short-term summer mission to Africa several years ago. She spent seven weeks in Mozambique, one of the poorest countries in the world, caring for orphans. Abby was most impressed by the warmth and affection of the African believers she met and described her observations of a tiny thatched-village church. She described the care and love expressed physically by the congregation for the babies during the long church service. The infants literally would be passed from lap to lap during the service, making their way around the entire congregation. The African proverb "It takes a village to raise a child" took on new meaning for all of us! Our experiences in other cultures have confirmed our growing conviction that Americans are touch-starved and are paying a significant price for this deprivation.

Numerous research studies confirm our anecdotal observations and conclusions. One landmark study was conducted several decades ago by Sidney Jourard, a University of Florida psychologist. Journard went to cafés in various cities around the world to observe and record the number of times two people drinking coffee together touched. The number of touches per hour was 0 in London; 2 in Gainesville, Florida;

110 in Paris; and 180 in San Juan, Puerto Rico.[2] Studies of touch among American parents and children, and among children and their peers, also document our touch deprivation. In one study, researchers went to McDonald's restaurants in Paris and Miami to assess parent/child interaction, particularly touch. They found that the American mothers touched their children only 3 percent of the time, whereas the French mothers touched their children 19 percent of the time—more than six times more than the Americans. The American children were, however, nineteen times more aggressive toward their mothers.[3] Studies of adolescents also reveal that American youth, even best friends, touch each other infrequently, as little as 2 percent of the time, but are much more likely to touch themselves and to be aggressive toward others than youth in other cultures.[4] Other research, including a comparison study of forty-nine different cultures, reveals that violence in a given culture can be directly correlated (in inverse relationship) with touch.[5] The authors of these studies explain this inverse relationship between touch and violence in terms of the long-term deleterious effects of touch deprivation.

Could it be that this affection deprivation helps explain why so many American adolescents are sexually active by age eighteen (85 percent of males and 77 percent of females)[6] and are increasingly inclined to be involved in "hookups," i.e., impersonal, noncommittal, and often anonymous sexual relations? In fact, our American youth are so starved for nonerotic touch that some have creatively structured affection for themselves and each other through "cuddle parties." This is a popular new social network created by two young professionals from New York. Cuddle parties take place across the U.S., Canada, and a few other industrial nations. They are organized social events or workshops designed to facilitate personal relational growth through consensual, nonsexual, affectionate touch expressed in individual and group hugs, handholding, backrubs, etc., with strict guidelines, including no alcohol or drugs, no

2. Jourard, "An Exploratory Study." For an excellent discussion of touch in various cultures, see Montagu, *Touching*, 292–392.

3. Field, "Preschoolers in America."; Field et al., "Behavior State Matching."

4. Field, "American Adolescents Touch Each Other Less."

5. Prescott, "Body Pleasure and the Origins of Violence"; Prescott, "Early Somatosensory Deprivation."

6. Alan Guttmacher Institute, "Teen Sex and Pregnancy."

pressure (you don't have to cuddle anyone with whom you are uncomfortable), and no sexual touch ("pajamas stay on the whole time").[7]

In spite of our wealth and abundance, we are touch-deprived. For many of us, this makes building healthy, nonerotic touch in our adult opposite-sex relationships nonintuitive. There are several factors that contribute to our discomfort around touch.

Tentative Masculinity

Many men have come to feel tentative or even insecure in their masculinity, so they bolster their sense of masculinity by tenaciously avoiding or denying what they perceive as feminine qualities such as emotional expression, acknowledging weaknesses, or any relational experience of vulnerability. The latter is particularly avoided by many men as a sign of weakness. This might well explain the peculiar findings of studies on touch among hospital patients. For example, numerous studies have shown the healing power of touch for those who are ill. In carefully controlled studies, touch by nurses, caregivers, and massage therapists has been shown to improve dramatically the wellbeing of nursing home patients; reduce blood pressure, pain, and nausea in cancer patients (by as much as 50 percent); stimulate premature newborns to gain 47 percent more weight; and significantly boost the immune systems of HIV-positive adults.[8] Curiously, preoperative women who are touched by nurses experience lower anxiety and have lower blood pressure in the recovery room, but preoperative men touched by nurses experience greater anxiety and have higher blood pressure in the recovery room.[9] The researchers of the study postulated that this dramatic gender-differentiated response might be the result of hospitalized men feeling more vulnerable when touched. Similarly, we have worked with many husbands whose wives expressed their desperation for physical affection, yet the husbands shrugged off this request by essentially denying the need for intimate touch with the declaration, "I'm just not the affectionate type!" This male bravado not only masks their own need for affection, but harshly invalidates their wife's intimacy needs as well. Perhaps the researchers are correct in pos-

7. www.cuddleparty.com.

8. Bush, "The Use of Human Touch"; Cassileth and Vickers, "Massage Therapy for Symptom Control"; Field et al., "Tactile/kinesthetic Stimulation Effects"; Ironson et al., "Massage Therapy"; Kinney et al., "Therapeutic Massage and Healing Touch."

9. Fisher and Gallant, "Effects of Touch on Hospitalized Patients."

tulating that, for some men, affectionate touch can trigger feelings of weakness and vulnerability that must be overcome.

Impact of Abuse

Abuse is a tragic, all-too-common reality in our society. Research shows that 30 to 40 percent of girls and 13 percent of boys experience childhood sexual abuse.[10] One out of five high school girls reports being physically or sexually assaulted by a male partner,[11] and 22 to 33 percent of North American women will be assaulted by an intimate partner in their lifetime.[12] Such widespread abuse poisons the well[13] of nourishing, affectionate touch, making it difficult for abuse survivors to offer or receive healthy touch. As an example, we have talked with numerous women who could not receive affectionate touch from their loving husbands, even though they were finally in a safe, caring relationship and their husbands' touch was kind and gentle, not abusive.

It is also important to note that, as our society has begun to acknowledge and address the reality of abuse, a harmful backlash has occurred. An overly cautious response to the dangers of "bad touch" has developed—a withholding of healthy, appropriate touch altogether. As an example, some childcare centers have gone so far as to instruct their staff to not pick up the children. Similarly, many schools have extensive policies prescribing and limiting the touch teachers can give children. Several years ago, when the president of the National Education Association appeared on the Oprah Winfrey show, she declared their slogan to be, "Teach, Don't Touch."[14] The sad result of misguided restrictions on healthy touch is that we are even more touch-deprived as people, and therefore increasingly uncomfortable giving or receiving affection.

---

10. These figures are based on a meta-analysis of twenty-two American studies using both national and regional sampling data: Bolen and Scannapieco, "Prevalence of Child Sexual Abuse."

11. Silverman et al., "Dating Violence against Adolescent Girls."

12. Eigengerg, *Women Battering in the United States*, 62–85; Tjaden and Thoennes, *Prevalence, Incidence, and Consequences of Violence against Women*; Siegel et al., "Screening for Domestic Violence."

13. For a more thorough explanation of this concept see Tracy, *Mending the Soul*.

14. Field, *Touch*, 3.

Impact of Pornography

Pornography has a devastating impact on affectionate touch. In a diabolically clever "bait and switch," pornography has everything—and nothing—to do with touch. On the surface, it appears to be the ultimate expression of unblushing touch—skin is revealed from head to toe and the participants seem to touch in every way imaginable. But, do they really touch?

Pornography subtly distorts affectionate touch in two primary ways: Firstly, all touch becomes eroticized touch. Particularly in the short term, pornography hypersexualizes its viewers. Libido is supercharged and the slightest affectionate touch is quickly eroticized. I (Steve) once ministered to a young man who came for counseling due to struggles in his dating relationship. For several years, off and on, he had been dating a committed Christian woman he had come to love deeply. They had similar values and interests and enjoyed each other immensely. In fact, he felt she might be the woman God wanted him to marry. He desperately desired to deepen their relationship, but felt strangely blocked in his efforts. During our first session, he disclosed struggles with pornography beginning in early adolescence. He wondered if the pornography was somehow related to his dating difficulties, though not in an obvious manner. This couple had maintained their sexual purity with each other. In fact, they had engaged in almost no physical contact whatsoever. I questioned more deeply, carefully constructing his family and sexual histories. It soon became clear why he felt stymied in his efforts to deepen their intimacy. He was absolutely petrified by any and all forms of affectionate touch. This was not hard to understand. As a part of his history, he recounted recent experiences with his three-year-old niece, and even his own mother, where normal affectionate touch initiated by them unleashed an internal firestorm of sexual desire and lewd fantasies. One of the primary factors in this tragic response was his chronic usage of pornography. He had unwittingly programmed his mind to eroticize all touch, so, therefore, to "keep the demons at bay," he had to shut down his heart and become physically stoical in all his relationships.

Secondly, pornography programs selfish touch, not a touch that gives. Very quickly, the user begins to touch as a way to take and loses the ability to touch in a way that expresses and gives love. Clearly, this "take touch" fragments the very foundation of a loving relationship—nurturing and affectionate touch that feels like love, that expresses love.

Pornography quickly conditions men to view women as mere objects for their own gratification. Hence, touch becomes all about grabbing, getting, taking, and not about tenderly giving. The late Andrea Dworkin, a brilliant and deeply wounded secular feminist, spent most of her adult life crusading against male oppression in all forms, including pornography. In her typically bare-knuckled style, she pares pornography down to its objectifying essence:

> The word *pornography* does not mean "writing about sex" or "depictions of the erotic" or "depictions of sexual acts" or "depictions of nude bodies" or "sexual representations" or any other such euphemism. It means the graphic depiction of women as vile whores. In ancient Greece, not all prostitutes were considered vile: only the *porneia*. Contemporary pornography strictly and literally conforms to the word's root meaning: the graphic depiction of vile whores, or in our language, sluts, cows . . . c—s. . . . Whores exist to serve men sexually. Whores exist only within a framework of male sexual domination.[15]

We must not allow the crude debasing touch of pornography to have the last word on the subject, for God has "wired" our bodies for *healthy, giving* touch.

BIOLOGY OF TOUCH

Touch is truly essential for physical and mental wellbeing from the cradle to the grave. Tiffany Field, a leading expert on touch and touch therapy, cites dozens of studies, including many of her own, that demonstrate the power of touch.[16] While researchers have known that touch is essential for relational and mental health, only recently have we come to understand the mechanisms that bring this about. One hormone in particular, oxytocin, is most critical in this process. Oxytocin is known as the "cuddle hormone."

Touch stimulates the production of this hormone and, thus, promotes a desire to touch and be touched. It makes us feel good about the person who causes the oxytocin to be released. Oxytocin promotes bonding. In fact, some of the early oxytocin research was promoted by

15. Dworkin, *Pornography,* 200.

16. Field, *Touch,* 131–51. Field is now the director of the Touch Research Institute at the University of Miami School of Medicine. The Institute's Web site (http://www6 .miami.edu/touch-research) gives updated abstracts of various touch research studies.

the desire to understand the differences in mating behaviors in voles, small grassland rodents. Researchers have discovered that oxytocin plays a decisive role in vole (and human) bonding and monogamy and helps explain why the prairie vole, the only type of vole to produce oxytocin, is the only monogamous, pair-bonded type of vole.[17] It also increases testosterone production, which results in greater sexual receptivity and libido by increasing the sensitivity of the penis and the nipples, improving erection, and making orgasms stronger. It may also increase sperm count. For women, oxytocin increases the production of estrogen, and these oxytocin effects are increasingly powerful as estrogen levels rise. This explains why women respond to the same touch differently at different times of the month. When the estrogen is high (ovulation), even a slight touch can have a strong effect; when estrogen is low (menstruation), it will take more touch to get the same sexual responses.

Oxytocin also inhibits the development of tolerance in the opiate receptors of the brain, helping to maintain sexual satisfaction in a bonded relationship.[18] As a relationship develops over time, fewer endorphins are released. However, oxytocin helps maintain the "wow" even with fewer endorphins, since sexual excitement is partially created by endorphins that excite the opiate receptors in the brain. This explains how a happily married, well-bonded couple will keep enjoying sex year after year, whereas a sex addict must keep raising the level of sexual stimulation to obtain the same level of satisfaction.[19] What is the moral of this story? Touch and be touched affectionately, until it is your most comfortable language of love.

Finally, oxytocin positively supports a couple during times of stress and conflict by decreasing mental processes and impairing memory; it promotes trust. Research studies in which some of the participants are given a nasal spray of oxytocin reveal that oxytocin dramatically increases people's sense of trust in others by as much as eighty percent, including trust in strangers.[20] Thus, it is important for couples to real-

17. Carter, "Oxytocin and Sexual Behaviour"; Carter, DeVries, and Getz, "Physiological Substrates of Mammalian Monogamy."

18. Hiller, "Speculations"; Johnson, "Emotions and the Brain: Love."

19. Oxytocin levels are at the highest during sexual arousal and orgasm (levels increase three to five times), during childbirth, and when a woman nurses.

20. Kosfeld et al., "Oxytocin Increases Trust in Humans"; Zak, Stanton, and Ahmadi, "Oxytocin Increases Generosity in Humans."

ize that, when they are in conflict and most tempted to back away from each other, literally and figuratively, they must resist this temptation and continue to move toward each other with tenderness, including tender touch.

BIBLICAL TOUCH

The propriety and importance of nonerotic, affectionate touch is a thoroughly biblical concept. In fact, numerous biblical texts describe affectionate touch that is so lavish it makes many of us uncomfortable. Males are often much less comfortable offering affectionate touch, so we do well to reflect carefully on the examples of biblical characters and let them challenge us to consider how we physically connect with friends and family. Christ gives us the quintessential biblical example of extravagant, affectionate touch. He frequently gave affectionate touch to those to whom he ministered, including children and those in great need.[21] Though Jesus had the power to heal at a distance, he rarely did.[22] Instead, healings occurred when Jesus touched the sick or they touched him.[23] Offering gracious physical touch was so important to Christ that he deliberately did it even when it created considerable physical or social risks. He touched lepers and allowed a "sinful woman" to caress his feet and dry them with her hair (Matt 8:1–3). Simon the Pharisee criticized Jesus for allowing such a passionate expression of affectionate love. Affectionate touch in the form of a kiss was so typical in Jesus' interactions with his disciples that Judas used it as a sign to identify him so his enemies could arrest him (Matt 26:48). In such a context, one would clearly select a sign that reflected normal, customary behavior that would not alarm the one about to be seized. Jesus was apparently comfortable with sustained nonerotic touch, for, during the final Passover meal, the "disciple Jesus loved" (John) "was reclining on Jesus' breast."[24]

21. Matt 19:15; 20:32–34; Mark 10:13–16.

22. John 4:46–53 and Matt 8:5–13 are among the few instances of Jesus healing at a distance, and the latter example was not initially going to be a distance healing.

23. Matt 8:1–3, 15; 20:32–34; Mark 6:5; 8:22–23; Luke 6:19; 8:42–48, 54.

24. John 13:23 NASV. The Greek phrase used here is translated literally by Andrew Lincoln who says the beloved disciple was "reclining in Jesus' lap"; *The Gospel according to John,* 378. Some translations such as the NRSV and NIV say the beloved disciple reclined not on Jesus' chest, but next to him. The difference in translation comes from the fact that the Greek preposition used here (*en*) has a wide range of meanings, including "in," "on," and "near"; Danker, *A Greek-English Lexicon,* 326. These translation varia-

There are certainly many other biblical examples of godly, healthy individuals such as Joseph, David, and Paul kissing and embracing family members and close friends.[25] Finally, we should note that, based on various New Testament passages, "ritual touch" has been incorporated in Christian church traditions in the form of "laying on of hands" for commissioning to ministry, foot washing, and the "holy kiss."[26]

While touch comes quite naturally to some, we know that, for others, it can be awkward. Typically, we are comfortable with the quality and frequency of affectionate touch that we grew up receiving. This explains why there is a learning curve for many of us when it comes to offering and receiving affection. A humorous example of a young married couple we counseled comes to mind. They had been married for several years, and she had grown increasingly dissatisfied with their relationship. When her relational unhappiness began to affect their sexual intimacy, he agreed to seek counseling with her. Early in our work together, as we were addressing their need as a couple for affectionate touch to be a consistent and frequent part of their loving, apart from sex, he began to look very puzzled. He asked us to describe what this touch might look like, and I eagerly gave him examples. After several minutes of reflection, his face lit up, and he exclaimed (in all seriousness), "Oh . . . I get it—It's like petting the dog!" The good news is that anyone can learn to give and receive nonerotic affectionate touch! Let's break down the steps into Morris's three stages.

---

tions are not as significant as it might appear, given the fact that, in Jewish custom, the disciples were reclining side by side, close to each other, so, when John spoke to Jesus, he would have turned back and essentially leaned on Jesus' chest.

25. Gen 45:14–15; 46:29; 1 Sam 20:41; Acts 20:36–38; cf. also Ruth 1:14; Luke 15:20; John 20:27.

26. Cf. Acts 6:6, 13:3; 1 Tim 4:14; 5:22; John 13:1–17; Rom 16:16; 1 Cor 16:20; 1 Thess 5:26; 1 Pet 5:14.

Stage Seven: Face to Face

I am my beloved's and my beloved is mine.
—Song 6:3

The physical dimension encompasses the previous emotional and relational dimensions of bonding. At this stage, the couple is deepening their ability to experience each other, to touch and be touched in physical and emotional ways. This stage begins the physically intimate sequence of bonding, and its metaphor is a kiss.

We are in such a hurry as people. It is difficult for us to slow down in our relationships long enough to make eye contact, to not only see, but to touch each other, physically and emotionally, throughout our day. The following story, as told by a young single woman in our ministry, describes the powerful role of physical touch, not only for intimacy, but also for healing. We will be unable to heal from the relational wounds we have experienced if we don't give and receive nurturing touch. As we offer touch in a face-to-face context, we not only give love to another, but also receive love in return.

Here is Julie's story. She lives in a highly social, predominantly Mexican community and describes loving it because:

> People are out, I know my neighbors' faces and they know mine. We know each others' names. . . . One of my most profound experiences was with a homeless man at a convenience store. I try to pray and obey the Spirit's prompting regarding how he would have me engage with the homeless on any given day. On this particular day, I asked this rather dirty and unkempt man to hold on a second as I placed my things in my car and grabbed some money to give him. As I returned I extended my hand to meet him, asked for his name (Daniel), and let him know I would be praying for him. As I did this, he held my hand just a little longer than is typical in these interactions. My gut was not concerned (perhaps because it was late morning and many were around, but more likely because my spirit sensed his genuine need), and I began to engage Daniel in conversation. I learned about his history, including that he had been homeless for some time, but in the next day or two he was to be placed in a subsidized unit for the seriously mentally ill. I celebrated with him and told him how thrilled I was for him! We talked a bit about Jesus and how we can trust Him in everything. I needed to go due to scheduled appointments, but Daniel held on to my hand. I covered his hand with my other hand as I looked into his eyes and saw such pain and brokenness. Tears welled in my eyes as he almost whispered, "I don't want to let go." I responded, "I know, Daniel, I know. I will be praying for you." I held on to his hand a moment longer, and then had to turn to go.
>
> I got in my car with tears spilling over and waved to Daniel as I backed away. . . . I knew deep within my soul what Daniel meant. This was not a man who had some perverse reason for not wanting to let go of my hand. This was a man who longed for the healthy, human touch for which we are designed by our Creator God, by our Abba Father. As I pursued my own journey of healing from abuse, neglect, and being used over and over, I did not allow any human touch when I felt at all vulnerable, and any touch that I did allow at other times I was not connected to. I had been devoid of healthy, human touch to which I could connect for over thirty years. When I finally began to allow this touch in, by Abba's grace and miraculous healing, my own soul and heart screamed out, "Please don't let go!" even though I cognitively knew that the

person needed to let go, not because of me, but simply because of life—the exact reason I needed to let go of his hand as he so painfully whispered, "I don't want to let go." I prayed that this small touch he received from my hands and heart and ultimately from our Abba Daddy, our Savior God, will lead him to God, to help him to experience God's love and care for him, and heal one of the many scars on his heart—just as each healthy, safe, loving, and nurturing touch is doing for me.

Touch continues to be a critical need all of our lives. Julie, the homeless in her neighborhood, and the rest of us need to give and receive touch. We are made for it; it heals us and points us to the healing touch of God.

Expand Your Touch Menu

Let him kiss me with the kisses of his mouth!
For your love is better than wine,
Your anointing oils are fragrant,
Your name is perfume poured out. . . .
Draw me after you, let us make haste.

—Song 1:2–4

A kiss can be a comma, a question mark, or an exclamation point. That's basic spelling that every lover ought to know.

—Mistinguett

Get excited about the incredible power you have in your partner's life through touch, and expand your touch repertoire. An enjoyable way of doing so that we have found through our three decades of marriage is to focus on kissing.

The most sensitive areas of skin on the human body are the "tips of the fingers, the clitoris, the tip of the penis, the tongue and the lips."[27] This helps us to understand why the lips need to be used a great deal in intimate bodily contact. An affectionate kiss is a most powerful way to communicate love and deepen intimacy. We enjoy "collecting" various kinds of kisses and their subsequent meanings. As a fun example, the words "cable car" take us back to our twentieth anniversary getaway to San Francisco. We had enjoyed a long day of touring, all on foot, and decided to take the shiny red cable car home. It was packed as we climbed

27. Morris, *Intimate Behoviour,* 129.

in, squeezing ourselves to the front of the aisle—we were wedged face to face. Tired and giddy, we began the lurching ascent up California Street. You see, I (Celestia) am the spontaneous and extroverted half of our relationship, and couldn't resist the temptation of planting the biggest kiss on my embarrassed husband the first time the conductor

> Kiss (kis) vb. 1. (tr.) to touch with the lips or press the lips against as an expression of love, greeting, respect, etc. 2. (intr.) to join lips with another person in an act of love or desire. 3. To touch (each other) lightly. ~n. 4. A caress with the lips. 5. A light touch.
>
> —Miriam Webster Dictionary

changed gears and pitched us, literally, into each other. Following this, a force came over me that I cannot explain, and I realized that I was in a most empowered position, knowing his arms were pinned, to kiss him every time the cable car lurched. We "cable car kissed" all the way home! Imagine three decades of collecting kisses and memories like this—one could write a book! You get the picture. Have fun practicing.

It is also interesting to note that we are commanded to kiss as an expression of love in friendship: "Greet one another with a holy kiss."[28] For those of us who are uncomfortable with affectionate kissing and "face-to-face" touching, we must practice until we are not! Face-to-face affection takes a couple to a much deeper level of intimacy, because face-to-face intimacy requires trust so that deeper levels of vulnerability can be tolerated and then enjoyed. Some women, for instance, will allow mouth to genital contact, but never mouth to mouth. If you are engaging in genital sex with your spouse, but not face-to-face affection, we encourage you to assess your sense of safety within the relationship, not just physically, but emotionally and sexually.[29] If you do feel safe with your spouse, then it is important to talk about your feelings and needs within the relationship. You can use the following questions and exercises as a starting point. Remember that affection, separated from

28. Rom 16:16.

29. If you do not feel safe within your relationship, it is important that you seek support and receive help in setting boundaries. God's plan is that you experience safety and comfort in your intimate relationships. If you are having difficulty trusting, there is a reason for that, and a trained counselor can help you. For additional help and support, visit our Web sites, www.mendingthesoulministries.org and www.globalhoperesources.org.

sex, in the context of a committed relationship, is an essential part of bonding and loving each other.

Exercises and Questions for Reflection and Sharing: Face to Face

1. Reflect on your childhood and the ways in which your family touched each other. What did you see modeled between your parents? How did they (or didn't they) touch you and your siblings? What are your touch memories between you and your siblings? Set apart some time that is unhurried and uninterrupted and share these stories with each other (Both the good and bad memories are important to share).

2. Describe your first kiss. What was the setting and how did it make you feel? How did it change your relationship?

3. When was the last time you kissed your spouse? Within your relationship, how often do you give or receive face-to-face affection in the course of a day? Describe the changes in face-to-face affection that you would like to see made in your relationship. Make one specific request of each other.

4. Read Song of Solomon 5:9–16 together. Notice how the wife speaks about her husband and describes him in poetic detail. Take turns answering the questions in verse 9 about each other, and then describe what you enjoy most about each other's bodies.

5. Set aside some quiet time for yourselves and kiss for one minute. Pay attention to your fuller sensory experience. Describe your thoughts and emotions to each other after kissing. Do it again. Talk about the meaning behind your kiss. What do you want each other to know?

6. Think about the commitment you are ready to make to your spouse regarding affectionate touch. What do you need? What do they need? How can you specifically increase the frequency of face-to-face affection on a daily basis? Write down your commitments for each other.

7. Take turns praying for each other. Stay face to face.

Stage Eight: Hand to Head

Set me as a seal upon your heart,
As a seal upon your arm;
For love is strong as death, passion fierce as the grave.
Its flashes are flashes of fire, a raging flame.
Many waters cannot quench love, neither can floods drown it.
If one offered for love all the wealth of one's house,
It would be utterly scorned.

—Song 8:6–7

By studying the behaviour of infants and lovers, it becomes clear
that the degree of physical intimacy that exists between two human animals relates to the degree of trust between them.

—Desmond Morris[30]

The frenzy of modern life creates anxiety and feelings of insecurity. The
pressure we feel to "keep up" deepens our levels of stress and fractures
our relationships, driving us to work harder and longer, removing us
from each other and furthering our isolation and relational fragmenta-

30. Morris, *Intimate Behaviour*, 145.

tion. Intimacy calms these feelings. Intimacy slows us down. Intimacy feeds us and focuses us again on what is most important. So, as hard as our hurried culture pushes us apart, we must push back toward each other creating daily, focused blocks of time.

When our children were young and we were living on a very tight budget, we would save all year for our one week of vacation as a family. We still remember our fantastic feelings of freedom when, for that one wonderful week, we had no financial worries. Our cash had been saved and was set aside for this particular time together, and we would do what we wanted, eat what and when we wanted, and even order drinks in restaurants! By saving and planning, we had carved out this stress-free zone for each other. We logged many memories during these scheduled vacations—experiences that we will never forget.

We suggest intentional margin for every couple. Think of the daily time you create and schedule into your marriage, as a mini-vacation that you enjoy together every day—time in which you listen, comfort, touch, and caress each other. We call this time, this daily vacation, our *sensate hour.*

The Sensate Hour

Sensate hour is the time reserved for the two of you, ideally the last hour of every day. Each of the five senses is involved in the focus on and enjoyment of each other.[31] As our lives became busier and we were increasingly extended in ministry, we gradually developed this routine to aid us in focusing on each other in a systematic and daily fashion. This time became part of our relational protection and intentional margin.

We suggest you set apart a room (typically the bedroom, because of the privacy and freedom from distraction) for the purpose of being with each other. During this time, you will experience each other through your God-given senses: affectionate touch, sound, smell, sight, and taste. It is helpful to explore your favorite genre of music, fragrances, textures, and colors so that you can build into your bedroom everything that images you as a couple, and place outside your bedroom anything that dis-

---

31. Lest some readers are tempted to say that they do not have time to focus on each other for a whole hour each day before bed, we should note that we developed our sensate hour routine years ago when Steve was in graduate school and we were both working and raising three children.

tracts you from each other.[32] In a sense, you are creating a new template of associations for comfort, safety, and love for each other. The rationale for selecting specific fragrances that are *only* used in the bedroom is that those scents become paired with current experiences of relational safety, comfort, attention, and love. In time, this becomes a powerful and comforting neurological association that helps to mitigate previous destructive sexual experiences and memories. For example, we collect various albums and artists that we only play during our sensate time together. Each musician and song is connected to warm memories for us that release powerful feelings of safety and love when we are together.

Creatively touch each other in ways that are both pleasurable and comforting. Lay your partner's head in your lap and focus your hands and lips on his face and head. Run your fingers through his hair and pay attention to the scent of his skin. With your finger, slowly trace the curves of his face until you have memorized the shape of his head. As you do this, tell him what you love about him and connect with the meaning of having him in your life. Study the texture and feel of her skin. Look into her eyes and trace her brows with the tip of your finger. Run your hand through her hair and lay her head softly across your chest. Tell her about the first time you noticed her and how she made you feel. While you hold and caress her head, tell her your favorite memories of being with her. When you think of her face, what do you see? Tell her. Close your eyes and touch his face. When you feel his cheeks and lips, what are you thankful for? How does he use his mouth to bless and encourage you? Tell him how thankful you are he is your husband; speak of your dreams for the future. What do you want him to know and never forget? Love him with your hands, your lips, and your words. Hold nothing back.

The literature tells us that hand-to-head contact is four times as common between young lovers as between older married couples. We challenge you to change those statistics and see what happens! Remember, touching begets more touching.

The sensate hour is designed to provide for the two of you an atmosphere for bonding to occur—deeply focused and intentional connecting. While the sensate hour is not designed for sex *per se,* it creates the environment for regular sexual intimacy to occur. The critical aspect of

32. We have found it helpful to keep our bedroom the room that is uniquely about us, and, therefore, hang our children's pictures, etc., in the hall outside our bedroom. We also suggest moving work stations, desks, televisions, etc., outside the bedroom.

this time together is to create an atmosphere for the first eight stages of the bonding sequence—emotional, relational, and physical touch. This sequence happens over and over again.

It is interesting to note that Morris analyzed several hundred illustrations in various sex manuals and found that only 4 percent of these illustrations showed any of the first eight stages. Eighty-two percent showed full copulation. The not-so-subtle message is: Bonding is all about copulation; sex is love and intercourse is bonding.[33] The sensate hour creates a time and place for the first eight stages. Customize this time for yourselves and enjoy your practice!

Exercises and Questions for Reflection and Sharing: Hand to Head

1. Would you like to incorporate a sensate hour into your daily schedule? What are your fears or concerns about doing so? Share these with each other.

2. If you are both in agreement, determine the time now that would best fit your schedule. The first hour of the day or the last? An afternoon? Think realistically and, if it is important to you both, put this time first into your busy schedules. What are the changes you will both need to make?

3. Are you both willing to completely "unplug?" Will you each make a commitment to turn off all cell phones, computers, televisions, etc., and keep them off? Are there any other requests you need to make of each other for your time together? If so, make them now.

4. Complete the following Sensate Templates. Rate from 0 (not at all) to 5 (I love it!) how much you enjoy the various kinds of affectionate touch on differing parts of your body. When you are done, share your templates with each other. Talk about the changes in the bedroom that you would like to make as a result of your combined templates. Make a plan!

---

33. Morris, *Intimate Behaviour*, 88.

Meditations for Her

> My lover is radiant and ruddy,
> Outstanding among ten thousand.
> His head is purest gold;
> His hair is wavy
> And black as a raven.
> His eyes are like doves
> By the water streams,
> Washed in milk,
> Mounted like jewels.

This ability to describe her lover's eyes in detail comes from holding eye contact and imprinting her brain with the memory of her lover's eyes and face. His response to her is to exclaim, "Turn your eyes from me; they overwhelm me." In other words, her eyes awaken in him such intensity of love that he is held captive.

> His cheeks are like beds of spice
> Yielding perfume.
> His lips are like lilies,
> Dripping with myrrh.
> His arms are rods of gold
> Set with chrysolite.
> His body is like polished ivory
> Decorated with sapphires.
> His legs are pillars of marble
> Set on bases of pure gold.
> His appearance is like Lebanon
> Choice as its cedars.
> His mouth is sweetness itself;
> He is altogether lovely.
> This is my lover, this is my friend,
> O daughters of Jerusalem.

—Song 5:10–16

HER SENSATE TEMPLATE

General Area	Location on Body	By Hands	By Mouth
Head and Face	Hair		
	Scalp		
	Lips		
	Ears		
	Forehead		
	Neck		
Torso	Stomach		
	Shoulders		
	Back		
Arms and Hands	Arms		
	Elbows		
	Wrists		
	Palms		
	Fingers		
Legs and Feet	Legs		
	Ankles		
	Feet		
	Toes		
Other			

Use the above template and rate from 0 (not at all) to 5 (I love it!) how much you enjoy the various kinds of affectionate touch on differing parts of your body.

Shade the boxes below that you prefer:

Textures	Scents	Colors
Cotton knit	Spicy/general	Black
Silk	Cinnamon	White
Satin	Musk	Cream
Netting	Sweet	Grey
Lace	Floral/general	Blues
Sheer	Rose	Greens
Flannel	Orange blossom	Yellows
Fur	Fresh clean sheets	Reds
Corduroy	Foods/general	Purples
Velvet	Vanilla	Oranges
	Cookie	
	Coffee	
	Wine	

Describe the genre of music you enjoy:

_____

_____

_____

List specific albums/songs/artists:

_____

_____

_____

How beautiful your sandaled feet,
O prince's daughter!
Your graceful legs are like jewels,
The work of a craftsman's hands.
Your naval is a rounded goblet
That never lacks blended wine.
Your waist is a mound of wheat encircled with lilies.
Your breasts are like two fawns,
Twins of a gazelle.
Your neck is like an ivory tower.
Your eyes are the pools of Heshbon
By the gate of Bath Rabbim.
Your nose is like the tower of Lebanon
Looking toward Damascus.
Your head crowns you like Mount Carmel.
Your hair is like royal tapestry;
The king is held captive by its tresses.
How beautiful you are and how pleasing,
O love, with your delights!

—Song 7:1–6

In this erotic poetry, Solomon describes his specific enjoyment and delight in his wife's body. He moves from the bottom of her feet to the top of her head.

His Sensate Template

General Area	Location on Body	By Hands	By Mouth
Head and Face	Hair		
	Scalp		
	Lips		
	Ears		
	Forehead		
	Neck		
Torso	Stomach		
	Shoulders		
	Back		
Arms and Hands	Arms		
	Elbows		
	Wrists		
	Palms		
	Fingers		
Legs and Feet	Legs		
	Ankles		
	Feet		
	Toes		
Other			

Textures	Scents	Colors
Cotton knit	Spicy/general	Black
Silk	Cinnamon	White
Satin	Musk	Cream
Netting	Sweet	Grey
Lace	Floral/general	Blues
Sheer	Rose	Greens
Flannel	Orange blossom	Yellows
Fur	Fresh clean sheets	Reds
Corduroy	Foods/general	Purples
Velvet	Vanilla	Oranges
	Cookie	
	Coffee	
	Wine	

Describe the genre of music you enjoy:

_____

_____

_____

List specific albums/songs/artists:

_____

_____

_____

After filling out each template, schedule a night out together in which you review your results with each other. Make a copy of each template and swap.

Stage Nine: Hand to Body

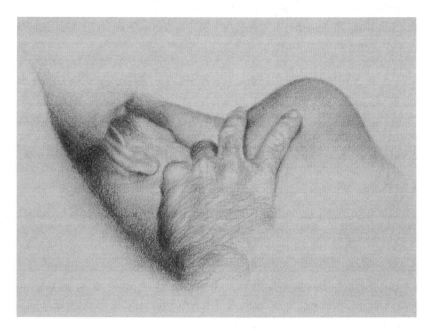

How beautiful you are, my love, how very beautiful!
Your eyes are doves behind your veil.
Your hair is like a flock of goats, moving. . . .
Your teeth are like. . . .
Your lips are like a crimson thread, and your mouth is lovely.
Your cheeks are like. . . .
Your neck is like the. . . .
Your two breasts are like. . . .
You are altogether beautiful, my love; there is no flaw in you.

—Song 4:1–7[34]

In this ninth stage, the sequence moves decidedly toward sex. If you as a couple do not have much history or practice with the first eight stages of bonding, we encourage you to take a month and keep your sensate time focused on the first eight stages. As you practice sexual restraint and enjoy this repeated bonding time together, you will begin to move toward what we call the experience of soul orgasm—the ignition

34. Use these verses for a hand-to-body template as your expression of love to each other.

of intense emotional sensations of bonding, being known and felt and experienced like you have never been before. This is a deeply enjoyable experience. Surprisingly, during the course of therapy, many men ask for this time of sexual restraint to be prolonged so that they can master this emotional and nonsexual bonding. Couples often express this sensate time to be invigorating and healing for them as individuals as well as for their relationship. Any couple can experience what every bonded couple knows—the more intimate the bond, the more fulfilling the sexual expression. In other words, sex gets better as a couple grows more intimate. There is great relief in the knowledge that our love does not depend upon the shape of our bodies or the exoticness of our sexual performance. Instead, our beautiful sexual expression flows out of the quality of our loving bond.

In summary, we will either meet these God-given needs of touch and comfort for each other, or we will be left to supplement them elsewhere. Thankfully, we have "professional intimacy givers" that, if used appropriately, do not unnecessarily compete with the relationship, but can supplement it. Most of us can attest to seeking out, at times, one or more of these comforters: counselor (emotional and spiritual comfort), massage therapist (nonerotic physical touch), beautician (head massage), manicurist (touch of fingers, hands, and arm), dance instructor (tender caress), coach, or even our pets.

In 2005, we were driving home from California after transitioning our twins into college dorms for their first full year of university. For us, September marked our first month of "empty nest." I (Celestia) remember crying all the way home on that long drive and mumbling, "It's all over. It's all over. It's all over. . . ." Steve listened incredulously and finally responded, "Honey, they are not dead!" All I knew at the time was that my heart and my arms felt an instant void that I was desperate to fill. Upon our arrival home, I immediately purchased two furry "babies"—a pair of darling, purring kittens to meet my needs for comfort and touch. My "big babies" were hundreds of miles away, so I brought home another set to take their place. I rocked those two kittens to sleep every evening, placing them in a basket for the night. My comfort routine continued until the evening they both simultaneously decided that they were done with that business and on to the bigger adventure of being full-grown cats!

We cannot deny our needs for deep, sensual, and intimate connection. Only our eternal Father could create a sensual, erotic, and passionate human love that would help us to experience more fully not only our originally designed selves, but ultimately God himself.

> Lip brushed eager lip—their bodies trembling
> In the breeze-kissed forest, touched.
> Terra blessed the warmth of first love.
> Closeness folded over in glorious assurance . . .
> I see Him even now within your eyes—
> His glory lights your hair.
> His warmth is in your touch.
> His trust walks in your footprints.
> His power calls me to give my body to your keeping
> As He gave you to me.
> Ask not if you shall meet Him.
> He swims the air we breathe—inhabits light.
> Unless your eyes should fail and all your senses die,
> You must meet Him, who can on any day,
> Fashion love from ordinary clay.[35]

Exercises and Questions for Reflection and Sharing: Hand to Body

1. Read aloud Song of Solomon 1:2, Genesis 45:14–15, and 1 Samuel 20:4. Discuss how the affectionate touch described in these verses is applicable to your relationship.

2. How comfortable are you with this "hand to body" stage of bonding? Explain.

3. On a scale of one to ten, how comfortable are you offering affectionate touch to your spouse and close friends? On a scale of one to ten, how well do you receive affectionate touch from your spouse and close friends? What negative feelings are stirred up inside you that inhibit your ability to give or receive healthy affectionate touch? What kinds of touch make you uncomfortable? Why?

4. Are there "ritual" touches that you would like to build into your marriage?[36]

35. Miller, *A Requiem for Love*, 40–42.

36. For instance, before meals, we hold hands, pray, and then kiss afterwards. This is a "ritual" touch that I grew up with in my family of origin that Steve and I decided to continue in our marriage.

5. Would you like to build into your schedules time for massage? Are their other kinds of hand-to-body touch you would like to experience with each other?

6. What is the best environment for you? What levels of privacy do you need to feel comfortable? Are there specific requests you need to make of each other? Do it now.

7. Make two lists of your needs for sensual/affectionate touch: "Inside the Bedroom" and "Outside the Bedroom." Create these lists individually and then share them with each other. Keep a copy of your spouse's list so that you can *do* something on that list every day for your partner. Practice these new touches until they are your comfortable routine. As a couple, you are developing your intimate, one-of-a-kind dance of love.

7

Sexual Dimension

Love's Magnificent Expression

I come to my garden, my sister, my bride; I gather my myrrh with my spice,
Eat, friends, drink, and be drunk with love.
—Song 5:1

THE VAST MAJORITY OF Christians value sex, believe it is a gift from
God, and consider it a vital aspect of marital love. These healthy
beliefs lead many young adults to assume mistakenly that vibrant
sexual intimacy automatically emerges in a loving Christian marriage.
Bill Hybels recounts his own naïve sexual expectations and experiences,
beginning with his honeymoon:

> For a week or two, it was to be a sexual paradise. That's the way
> we had pictured it. Florida, the hot sun, the beach, and, best of
> all, the bedroom. Pure ecstasy. After a victorious and difficult
> struggle to remain sexually pure before our marriage, Lynne and
> I were finally going to get what we deserved. Sex. And plenty of
> it. That was before some cosmic sense of humor kicked in. Our
> honeymoon was a disaster. . . . First came the sunburns. Severe
> ones. That kind that bring nausea, then blistering and peeling.
> Our cries of "I want you, I have to have you!" turned into "Don't
> you dare touch me!" While we were recovering from our sun-
> burns, Lynne developed a cold sore. Not just an average cold sore,
> mind you: it stretched from her lip to the middle of her neck.
> . . . I laughed about it. Lynne, not surprisingly, accused me of be-
> ing insensitive and didn't exactly feel like Cindy Crawford. That
> was our sexual debut.

> The early years of our marriage didn't exactly scorch the planet either. Due to our ignorance and circumstances, we did just about everything possible to eliminate sexual fulfillment. I was a full-time youth minister and a full-time college student. . . . Lynne had two full-term pregnancies, during which she was sick four to five times a day for nine months, and two pregnancies ending in miscarriages, during which she was just as sick. Add to that the all-too-common inability to communicate about sex, and you get the idea. When we were hot, it was often in anger, not passion. We lived like this for eight years.
>
> On our eighth wedding anniversary, I wanted to make up everything to Lynne. We would finally get to be the sexual dynamos we really were. With the help of a friend, who was the manager of a hotel, I planned an elaborate anniversary celebration. A veritable sexual feast. . . . At first, everything went according to plan. We had a romantic dinner together, and then, after checking into our hotel, we were awestruck with our room; it was the mother of all honeymoon suites: mirrors everywhere, a huge Jacuzzi and sauna, and, in the center of it all, a bed on a platform.[1]

After blowing out the candles, just before their anticipated "wild romance," Lynne accidentally walked into one of the bedpost mirrors, necessitating four stitches. Thus, their "passion was spent, not in a honeymoon suite but in the emergency room of a hospital."[2] Thankfully, this story didn't mark the end of sexual intimacy for Bill and Lynne, but the beginning. Lifelong, vibrant marital sexual intimacy can and does happen, but it won't happen automatically! Our sexuality is the best and most intricate part of who we are and can be derailed in countless ways.

GOD'S GOOD GIFT OF SEX: PATHWAYS OF LIFE[3]

The thief comes only to steal and kill and destroy;
I came that they may have life, and have it abundantly.

—John 10:10

Surely, one of Satan's most widespread, persistent lies is that one must go outside of God's commandments to find satisfaction because God's

---

1. Hybels and Wilkins, *Tender Love*, 81–82.

2. Ibid., 83.

3. Portions of this section are drawn from Tracy, "Chastity and the Goodness of God."

interests and our wellbeing are not aligned. This lie is particularly applicable to sexuality, where it often appears to us that we are more concerned with our sexual needs and fulfillment than God is. Hence, we are tempted to bypass God's directives to "take care of" ourselves. We must remember that Hugh Hefner didn't create sex, nor did Satan. Sex is God's magnificent handiwork! The loving Lord of the universe wove sexuality into the essential fabric of creation. He made us sexual beings with sexual drives and longings. He made our bodies with genitals filled with pleasure receptors. Thus, erotic expressions of sexuality are not an unintended consequence of creation, but precisely what he planned and created for married couples.

We read in chapter 1 that gender flows out of being made in God's image, for it gives us the longing and capacity for intimacy and God himself is intrinsically relational. Furthermore, marital sex can and should be one of the most beautiful, powerful expressions of our God-likeness and of God's love for us. We resonate with the way Dan Allender and Tremper Longman connect sexual intimacy in marriage with intimacy with God: "God loves sex. Married expression is a paradigm of his intimacy with his people. And the pleasure of arousal and climax are pictures of what God desires for his people not only in marriage but also in worship and praise of him."[4] There is much we would love to say about the divine purposes for marital sex, but the most important point is this: *God desires sex to express, celebrate, and deepen a couple's sacred love bond with each other and with himself.* Consider some of the ways loving marital sex can do this:

1. *Reproduction.* Sex is the very means by which the miracle of life takes place, allowing a couple to create a unique life through their physical expression of love.

2. *Pleasure.* Sexual pleasure culminating in orgasm is one of the most unique, intense delights that humans experience. Thus, it is an exquisite privilege for couples to give and receive pleasure through sexual union.

3. *Passion.* Sex has a transcendent, mystical quality unlike virtually any other human experience. In a loving marriage, sexual passion drives couples toward each other and deepens their bond.

---

4. Allender and Longman, *Intimate Allies,* 255.

4. *Delight.* Sexual passion creates a focus on and delight in our partner. This can be so intense that it seems the whole world stands still.

5. *Vulnerability.* Our sexuality encompasses some of the most personal and sensitive parts of our being. Healthy sexual intimacy involves physical and emotional exposure, creating a vulnerability that necessitates safety and trust.

6. *Symbol.* Married couples are to approach sex with their spouse as an act of worship. In the physical act of sexual intimacy, married couples symbolize, reaffirm, and strengthen the sacred one-flesh covenant they made to God and to each other.

It is encouraging to note that secular sexuality research evidences the wisdom and goodness of the biblical sexual ethic, namely, that sex is properly experienced only in marriage as a powerful, bonding expression of love. For instance, social science studies have found:

- Married couples report considerably higher rates of sexual satisfaction than singles, and, among women, conservative Protestant women have the highest rates of orgasm.[5]

- Married men and women experienced significantly more emotional satisfaction with sex than sexually active singles. In one study, married men were found to experience 60 percent higher emotional satisfaction rates from sex than single men experienced.[6]

- Married couples are two times more likely to be sexually faithful to their partners than cohabiting couples.[7]

- Marital sexual satisfaction is most strongly correlated not with sexual techniques, but with the overall wellbeing of the marriage, particularly with high levels of love and affection.[8]

Eros is kindled when we patiently wait and build a relationship from the inside to the outside. Marriage, then sex, is our soul seal.

5. Michael et al., *Sex in America,* 127–28; see also Richard, "Christian Women Have More Fun."

6. Waite and Joyner, "Emotional and Physical Satisfaction with Sex," 266.

7. Treas and Giesen, "Sexual Infidelity among Married and Cohabiting Couples," 59.

8. Hsiu-Chen et al., "Relationships Among Sexual Satisfaction, Marital Quality, and Marital Instability"; Young et al., "Sexual Satisfaction among Married Women."

THE GOD OF THIS WORLD: PATHWAYS OF DEATH

Eros ceases to be a devil only when it ceases to be a god.

—C. S. Lewis[9]

The wings of demons are as white as angels' wings.
Their halos are as golden bright.
They sing as well as angels too, but only when it's night.

—Calvin Miller[10]

Satan is a liar and a thief. Nowhere is this more poignantly clear than in our sexuality, where Satan steals physical, emotional, and spiritual life. Today, we are experiencing dramatic cultural shifts that are rewriting our experiences as men and women—our sexual expressions and our expectations. Our culture is now so saturated with sexual lies, particularly those that flow from pornography, that we have lost a natural sense of what loving, appropriate sexual expression looks like. Several secular writers have described the influence of pornography—particularly its portrayal of sex as mere physical copulation focused purely on one's own physical gratification, most often involving the degradation and domination of women—as a "pornification," which is transforming every aspect of our culture. Carmine Sarracino and Kevin Scott state this powerfully:

> Porn has so thoroughly been absorbed into every aspect of our everyday lives—language, fashion, advertisements, movies, the Internet, music, magazines, television, and video games—that it has almost ceased to exist as something separate from the mainstream culture, something "out there." That is, we no longer have to go to porn in order to get it. It is filtered to us, in some form, regardless of whether we want it or are even aware of it.[11]

Robert Jensen, a nonevangelical journalism professor who has thoroughly studied American sexual culture, sounds an ominous warning:

9. Lewis, *Christian Reflections*, 35.

10. Miller, *A Requiem for Love*, 128.

11. Sarracino and Scott, *The Porning of America*, x; see also Paul, *Pornified*. It is thus very sobering that a study of male sexuality conducted in the early 1990s, when pornography was less available and acceptable than it now is, found that 94 percent of the Christian men surveyed reported having been exposed to pornography, and only 6 percent of these men believed they had escaped its influence; Hart, *The Sexual Man*, 89.

There's an old adage: Allow me to write the stories that people tell, and I will not need to write the laws. . . . Pornography is telling us stories about what it means to be a man, to be a woman, to be sexual as men and women. Are these the stories we want told? Is this the world we want to build? At the moment it is a pornographers' world. They are the ones telling the most influential stories about gender and power and sex.[12]

We have a lot of reframing to do within our relationships to challenge these pervasive lies about gender, relationships, and sexuality. May we tell our honest stories about our experiences as men and women; may we listen with courage to each other in order to be changed by what we hear. May we create sensitive bonds between us that attune to each other's needs.

The sexual standards of our contemporary society have created artificial measures that purport to be realistic and right. Subtly, we have made these our guidelines instead of natural, organic sexual expressions within our unique relationship. Walter Wangerin reminds us of God's placement of sex within the whole of the relationship and warns of the dangers of what has become normalized within our bedrooms.

Yet the (cultural) fantasy becomes the goal of these individuals; and the goal becomes a standard; and when nothing matches the standard, they feel cheated. Instead of seeking what may be, they damn their spouses for what is not—or they attempt sexual acts, maneuvers, aids, advices, which are in fact unnatural. Unnatural, I mean, to their natures, the natures of their spouses and their relationships.[13]

Married couples must thoughtfully customize their lovemaking, being aware of the limits of healthy sexual expression in light of the direct and indirect influence of pornography. We have created the illustration below to visualize green-light sexual activities—those that are clearly healthy based on biblical principles; yellow-light sexual activities, which are often unhealthy and need to be cautiously evaluated based on individual needs; and red-light sexual activities—those that are unhealthy, inappropriate, and clearly violate biblical principles.

12. Jensen, *Getting Off*, 84–85.
13. Wangerin, *As For Me and My House*, 181.

GREEN LIGHT

MUTUALITY AND EQUALITY

[B]ecause of the temptation to immorality, each man should have his own wife and each woman her own husband. The husband should give to his wife her conjugal rights, and likewise the wife to her husband. For the wife does not rule over her own body, but the husband does; likewise the husband does not rule over his own body, but the wife does. (1 Cor 7:2–4)

Likewise you husbands, live considerately with your wives, bestowing honor on the woman as the weaker sex, since you are joint heirs of the grace of life, in order that your prayers may not be hindered. (1 Pet 3:7)

FREQUENT SEX

Husbands and wives have a sacred responsibility to regularly meet each other's sexual needs. (1 Cor 7:3)[14]

PASSIONATE SEX

Let your fountain be blessed, and rejoice in the wife of your youth, a lovely deer, a graceful doe. May her breasts satisfy you at all times; may you be intoxicated always by her love. (Prov 5:18–19)

CREATIVE SEX: EXPLORING AND ENJOYING EACH OTHER'S BODIES

[The man speaks.] How beautiful you are. . . . Your stature is like that of the palm, and your breasts like clusters of fruit. I said, "I will climb the palm tree; I will take hold of its fruit. May your breasts be like the clusters of the vine, the fragrance of your breath like apples, and your mouth like the best wine." [The woman speaks.] May the wine go straight to my lover, flowing gently over lips and teeth. I belong to my lover, and his desire is for me. (Song 7:6–10 NIV)

14. Author's paraphrase.

SHAMELESS SEX

[A]nd they become one flesh. And the man and his wife were both naked, and were not ashamed." (Gen 2:24–25)

SATISFYING SEX

Let him kiss me with the kisses of his mouth! For your love is better than wine. (Song 1:2)

EXCLUSIVE SEX

But because of the temptation to immorality, each man should have [sexual relations with] *his own* wife and each woman *her own* husband. (1 Cor 7:2, emphasis added)

You have heard that it was said, "You shall not commit adultery." But I say to you that everyone who looks at a woman with lust has already committed adultery with her in his heart. (Matt 5:27–28)

UNSELFISH, GIVING SEX

When a man takes a new wife, he shall not go out with the army nor be charged with any duty; he shall be free at home one year and shall give [sexual] happiness to his wife whom he has taken.[15] (Deut 24:5)

YELLOW LIGHT

ORAL SEX

Concern: We have no concern with oral sex as an aspect of foreplay, but oral sex as "sex" often fails the test of mutuality. (1) It often prioritizes the man's sexual fulfillment, his orgasm, over the woman's. (2) The connotation of oral sex, as sex performed on the man, particularly as symbolized

---

15. Old Testament scholar Richard M. Davidson argues that sexual pleasure is the focus of the "happiness" referred to in this verse; *Flame of Yahweh*, 505.

in pornography, is one of female inferiority. She kneels before him and services him, to the neglect of her sexual needs.

Cosmetic Surgery to Enhance Sex

Concern: Our pornified culture elevates sexual anatomy over personhood, creating an artificial and absurd standard of beauty which dishonors the spouse God providentially created and gave to us (Prov 19:14). Healthy marital sex comes from a loving, bonded relationship, not from surgically enhanced body parts. Husbands who pressure their wives to have painful, medically unnecessary cosmetic surgery to enhance their sex life are misguided and selfish.

Shaving (Woman's) Pubic Hair

Concern: While we would not argue that this common practice is intrinsically wrong, we are concerned about its implications. (1) Shaving pubic hair makes a woman's genitals appear prepubescent, which is precisely the perverted message often intended in pornography. (2) For the majority of women, negative body image is one of their greatest challenges, often adversely impacting sexual desire. It is essential that husbands assist their wives in affirming their bodies just as they are, as fearfully and wonderfully crafted by Almighty God (Ps 139:13–14).

RED LIGHT

Use of Pornography

Problem: Scripture is adamantly clear that sex is sacred and only to be enjoyed by two people who have made a covenant commitment to each other. According to Jesus, sexual lust toward someone you are not married to is a form of adultery. Unfortunately, the use of erotica (material that depicts graphic sexual acts in a "loving" and "mutually consenting" context) is a standard tool used by secular and often Christian counselors with married clients experiencing sexual struggles. Pornography can certainly provide a short-term sexual boost for couples, but it comes at great long-term, moral, and relational cost.

ANAL SEX[16]

Problem: God did not make the rectal muscles for sexual activity. They tear easily during sex, have no natural lubrication, and are filled with bacteria. The toxic contents of the rectum as well as the semen seeping through small fissures can cause serious health problems. God beautifully crafted our bodies, particularly our genitals, for sexual activity. He created the rectum for the elimination of bodily waste.

MASOCHISM, BONDAGE, OR DEGRADING SEXUAL PRACTICES

Problem: Sex is designed by God to express love, mutuality, and respect. Any sex act which literally *or symbolically* produces pain, degradation, or oppression is inappropriate and harmful.

COERCIVE SEX

Problem: Sex is to be mutually satisfying and mutually agreed upon. Any sexual practice that is coercive undermines love, trust, and respect. It is hostile to all that marital lovemaking should express.

The following questions may help a couple determine whether a specific sexual activity is healthy and appropriate.

1. Does it communicate love, respect, and equality?

2. Does it bring pleasure to both partners?

3. Does it express and enhance bonding and closeness?

Bless each other within marriage by taking the pressure off the sex act itself. Relax, talk, and create together—surrendering and serving one another as you understand each other's needs. Nothing is to be demanded or expected. Reject societal norms; look and listen to each other. Imagine and create your own expressions of love, attuning carefully to each other's needs and desires.

SEXUAL BONDING: THREE STAGES

We are now going to move into Morris's final stages of bonding, which comprise the sexual dimension of intimacy. It is difficult to address

16. Research suggests that cultural influences have caused anal sex to become much more widely accepted and practiced since the early 1990s. Some recent studies indicate that close to 40 percent of men and one-third of women have practiced anal sex; McBride and Fortenberry, "Heterosexual Anal Sexuality."

sexuality in marriage adequately in just a few short pages. However, the discipline requires us to focus on the essentials of sexual health and satisfaction. Sex therapists Cliff and Joyce Penner were asked to sum up their findings after thirty years of successful clinical practice. What they shared will probably surprise you. They state:

> Our most convincing finding is that men make the difference when it comes to sex in marriage. Because of the natural differences between men and women, we are convinced that the most vital factor in building intimacy and keeping passion alive in marriage revolves around ... the man. This is true whether he has a problem, she has a problem, or there is no problem.[17]

Men, we know this seems unfair, but it is God's model and mandate, not ours. We would like to paraphrase from Paul's marital instructions in Ephesians 5:21–33:

> The husband sacrificially loves, adores, and connects with his wife. She will see his willingness to sacrifice to the point of death if necessary in order to make her feel safe and cherished; his adoration allows her to believe in her beauty and open up sexually; his emotional energy and delight in her ignites her passion; she invites him into her heart and body sexually;[18] he feels validated, desired, and fulfilled, they both end up satisfied. It's a win-win! And the cycle of loving goes on and on.

17. Penner, *The Gift of Sex*, xii–xiii. This quote need not be understood in a hierarchical manner. That is not how we understand it.

18. Ibid., xii. We appreciated the Penners' paraphrase of Ephesians 5 and have expanded this concept. A woman is created to experience Ephesians 5 love, which ignites a sexual confidence in her that allows her to lead with her sexuality, believing in her right also to sexual pleasure and satisfaction in the marriage bed. This is a beautiful picture of mutuality in marriage that inverts the prescriptives of our sexualized culture.

Stage Ten: Mouth to Breast

How beautiful you are, my love, how very beautiful!
Your two breasts are like two fawns, twins of a gazelle
that feed among the lilies.
You are altogether beautiful, my love; there is no flaw in you.

—Song 4:1, 5–7

In this tenth stage of bonding, the focus is on the exploration of each other's bodies. This typically involves his enjoyment of her breasts as he fondles her with both his mouth and hands. "Mouth-to-breast contacts are the last of the pre-genital intimacies and are the prelude to actions which are concerned not merely with arousal, but with arousal to climax."[19]

As we have already explained, God's design for lovemaking[20] is within the context of covenantal, committed love. This means that both

19. Morris, *Intimate Behaviour,* 78.

20. By lovemaking, we mean the expression of bonded love. Love is not "made" by sex, but is expressed and "kept" through sex. The emphasis cannot be sex, but instead must be the quality of the relationship, and then this bonded intimacy will produce "good sex." In short, good sex does not create love, it expresses it.

partners are completely committed to each other for life, in a relationship of trust and total honesty. Safety, respect, and equality are relationally evident—they have no fear of being abandoned, hurt, or deliberately harmed. Both have confidence that the commitments made to each other are grounded in a mutual relationship with the Lord that is both individually and corporately nurtured. The focus is on the relationship itself, and sex becomes the expression of their committed love.

In their book *When Two Become One*, Chris and Rachel McCluskey articulate a simple model that combines both the emotional and relational dimensions of lovemaking with the physical and sexual.[21] Their four-cycle model collapses the four dimensions of intimacy that have been expanded within this book (emotional, relational, physical, and sexual) into a sexual framework within marriage. We recommend this model for couples wishing to simplify the twelve steps of bonding expanded in this book into a simpler model focused primarily on their sexuality.

Creating an Atmosphere for Lovemaking

PRIVACY

"Do we have enough privacy for lovemaking?" This is a question that you both must honestly answer. If the answer is no, the solution will take planning and careful execution. Technology has not only sped up our lives, but it has also invaded the privacy of every room in our homes! Today, we can have multiple phones ringing, portable wireless devices vibrating, and computers dinging all at the same time. As a result of this technological advancement, we do not have the natural boundaries around our personal space and relationships that we once enjoyed. Today, all privacy will have to be deliberately created. How will you focus your time together? What will be your guidelines around cell phones, computers, emailing, etc.? Do you want technology in your bedroom? How will you protect specific rooms of the house for relational privacy? What will your personal boundaries be around relational information exposed via the Internet on Facebook, in chat rooms, etc.?

Create and protect intimacy nights, coaching children and anyone else living with you that this is your time to focus on your relationship as a couple. You are not to be bothered. It is your task as a couple to provide

21. McCluskey, *When Two Become One*, 88–100.

privacy for yourselves frequently and at regular intervals, or your sex life will greatly suffer. You will be richly rewarded for this discipline. Not only will your relationship have the space it needs to develop and grow, but you also will be showcasing a beautiful model to others in an age of stressful, frenetic, disconnected activity. Relationships take time and energy to cultivate, and this cannot be done without focused and private time together.

FOCUSED AND PROTECTED ENERGY

"Do we have enough energy by the time we come together sexually?" This is one of the primary issues facing couples in Western culture today. Again, we must be intentional about what we *choose*, because, sadly, we really can't have it all! What are the good things we need to say no to in our marriage in order to prioritize energy for lovemaking? As a personal example of creating an intentional focus, we have included Celestia's Millenium Mission, written in the winter of 1999. We were entering our "decade of adolescents."[22] There was much at stake, and we didn't want to lose our way unintentionally because of the strong, competing distractions within our ministry and culture.

My mission is to live with love and integrity.
To profoundly impact the lives of others for God's kingdom.
I will do this as I make careful and calculated choices,
consistent with my deepest values.
I value my relationship with Jesus Christ and will seek
to balance my time in such a way as to prioritize that relationship.
This requires a quiet, focused time each day to
journal and reflect on God's word to me.
I will maintain a mentor in my life to guide,
support, and offer truth.
I will live each principle that I teach so I do not develop
a dissonance between who I think I am and who I really am.
I will remember every day the ease at which a heart can self-deceive.

22. Our three active, fun, and busy children were just entering their adolescence, and we were strongly aware that we were entering a decade in which we would need keen focus to keep our priorities straight. I (Celestia) wrote this mission and posted copies in our kitchen, my office, and in my journal. All five of us claimed a verse that would be our focus for the decade in front of us. We framed these verses beside my Millenium Mission on our family room wall as a daily reminder to remember the important things—which was, for us as a family, our relationships.

I value my relationship with my husband.
I will make choices about my time that consider him first.
I will schedule daily time at the beginning and
end of each day to reflect with him.
I will endeavor to share every feeling, thought, and
dream as I become aware of its significance.
I will work to make his needs and dreams as
important to me as they are to him.
I will seek to know him and to accept the man I find him to be.
I will offer the best of me.

I value my relationship with my children.
I will prioritize their emotional needs at the
same level as their physical needs.
I will remain faithful to prioritize my time in order
to be predictably available to them.
I will pray for them and with them on a daily basis
for God to be unleashed in their lives.
I will, with God's help, harness my fears about their safety
so I can say "Yes!" to God's call on their lives.
I will encourage risk-taking and passionate choices
in their service of God.
I will remember that they are ultimately His.

I value my relationship with others.
I will be respectful and kind when I do not feel
like being respectful and kind.
I will hold onto truth, but not at the expense of grace.
I will endeavor to set boundaries that protect my relationships
with people God has ordained to be in my life.
I will seek God's balance of mercy.[23]

TIME[24]

"Do we enjoy enough time together when we have *both* privacy and
energy?" Time cannot be created; it must be protected for what matters

23. Spencer and Tracy, *Marriage at the Crossroads*, 136–37.

24. In one study of marital satisfaction among 542 middle-aged married couples, the number-one thing the vast majority (78 percent) wished they could change was to be able to have more time together; Christensen and Miller, "Areas of Desired Change." Similarly, in a study of young married couples, "balancing job and family" and "frequency of sexual relations" were the top two reported problems; Risch, Riley, and Lawler, "Problematic Issues."

most to us. "Privacy, energy, and time are required if you are to luxuriate in sexual relations."[25] In the Relational Intimacy chapter, we suggested the guideline of providing for your relationship a minimum of fifteen hours per week in focused, attentive time with each other. Think of this focused time as making love throughout the day. It is your opportunity to express in emotional, verbal, and physical ways your delight in and enjoyment of your partner. It is the time spent pursuing each other—asking questions, sharing details of your days, dreaming, gardening, exercising, walking, laughing, planning, cooking, eating, hugging, kissing . . . you get the picture! Think of this daily investment of time as the prepared soil in which your love will grow.

SENSUAL

"Do we have privacy, energy, and time enough to enjoy regular sensual touch?" One of the most natural ways of enjoying this tenth stage of lovemaking, and the exploration of your partner's body, is through massage. Christian sex therapist Douglas Rosenau has a chapter in his excellent guidebook, A Celebration of Sex, dedicated entirely to sensuous massage. He notes that massage "has been shown to have profound effects on the one giving the massage as well as the person receiving it. A massage reduces stress, blood pressure goes down, and a relaxed, comfortable, nurturing atmosphere is encouraged within the companionship."[26]

In this tenth stage, couples are encouraged to focus on sensual touching—both partners being nude, comfortable, and relaxed. Most sex therapists encourage couples to set apart at least two fifteen-minute time periods during the week in which each partner takes turns initiating the massage. It is important to discuss parameters of the massage as a couple ahead of time so that expectations are clarified. For instance, some women will want breast stimulation to be a part of this massage and others will not. You are customizing your lovemaking, and therefore the sensual massage is a sensual expression developed and enjoyed together. The focus here is on enjoyment of each other and sensual touch without the "pressure" of sexual performance. For specific direction and illustrations, we highly recommend Rosenau's insightful book.

25. McCluskey, When Two Become One, 94.
26. Rosenau, A Celebration of Sex, 99–117.

Exercises and Questions for Reflection and Sharing: Mouth to Breast

1. Together, read the poetry of Song of Solomon 4:1–7, which is the man's sensuous description of the woman's beautiful body. Create your own poetry of affirming and sensuous descriptions of delight in each other. Share this directly with each other.

2. How comfortable are you with this mouth-to-breast stage of bonding? Explain.

3. What do you enjoy about the privacy you have already established in your relationship? Do you need to make any specific requests of each other in order to increase your privacy? If so, make them now.

4. On a scale of one to ten, rate the level of emotional/sexual energy you are currently experiencing from your partner. How does this affect your sexual desire and arousal? Do you have any specific requests to make of each other? If so, do it now.

5. How many relationally focused hours are you currently enjoying per week as a couple? Describe how this is impacting you sexually. How much time would you like to intentionally plan into your week for focused time as a couple? What changes do you need to make to create this new reality? What requests do you need to make of your partner?

6. Describe the difference that this adjustment in relationally focused time will make for each of you.

7. Create a plan! Grab a sheet of paper and sketch out a renewed plan for privacy, focused energy, time, and sensual massage in your marriage. Be specific, and include the changes that you are committing to make.

8. Kneel together and pray—dedicating your relationship and this stage of deepened sexual intimacy to the Lord. Pray for each other.

Stage Eleven: Hand to Genitals

Let my beloved come to his garden, and eat its choicest fruits.

—Song 4:16

While evangelicals have varied convictions regarding the specifics of innate biological differences between men and women,[27] they strongly agree that God made men and women diverse to complement each other. In the creation account, gender distinction is a foundation for marriage itself. God made a woman, Eve, from the man, yet distinct from him, so that she would complement him as an equal partner. Thus, Stanley Grenz describes Eve as a majestic female "counterpart" to Adam. Her sexual differentiation as a woman allowed her to bond with Adam, creating a one-flesh union, a beautiful antidote to Adam's isolation and loneliness.[28] Male/female sexual differences are fundamental to experiencing and enjoying God's gift of marriage and sex. As the French say, *vive la*

27. For a concise overview of two different evangelical understandings of biological gender differences, along with documentation of key sources, see Spencer and Tracy, *Marriage at the Crossroads*, 114–15, 127–31.

28. Grenz, *Sexual Ethics*, 32–33.

différence![29] At the same time, biological gender differences create some of the greatest challenges to sexual intimacy. Nowhere are these more obvious or dramatic than in the area of sex. Therefore, a couple's sexual intimacy is best built upon accurate knowledge of each other's unique sexual patterns and needs. This information is not intuitive and typically must be learned so that couples can more fully understand and, thus, respect each other.

Boys Are Not Girls: Gender and Marital Sexuality

One of the most extensive evangelical studies of female sexuality involved a survey of more than two thousand Christian women. This study resulted in the publication of *Secrets of Eve: Understanding the Mystery of Female Sexuality*,[30] and followed an earlier, similar study of evangelical male sexuality, published in the book *The Sexual Man*.[31] These two studies reveal seven common sexual gender differences.[32] These findings are descriptive, not prescriptive, since we are all unique individuals. We have found these identified differences to be broadly supported by other recent research studies.[33]

1. WE DIFFER IN HOW WE THINK ABOUT SEX.

Qualitatively and quantitatively, men and women think differently about sex. Qualitatively, husbands tend to be less satisfied with their marital sex lives, particularly the frequency of sexual relations, than wives. A surprisingly dominant question for all of the male survey respondents was, "Am I normal?" The women, however, were most often troubled about whether their sexual desire/interest was abnormally low, whereas men were overwhelmingly concerned that they were abnormally "oversexual." Quantitatively, men think about sex *much* more often than women. One earlier famous study found that, on average, males ages twelve to forty think about sex six times per hour (more than seven hundred times per

29. This literally means, "long live the difference."

30. Hart, Weber, and Taylor, *Secrets of Eve*.

31. Hart, *The Sexual Man*.

32. Hart, Weber, and Taylor, *Secrets of Eve*, 252–57; see also Hart, *The Sexual Man*, 67–68.

33. Fisher, *Why We Love*, 79–83, 198–201; Hiller, "Speculations"; Meltzer and McNulty, "Body Image and Marital Satisfaction"; Meston and Buss, *Why Women Have Sex*, 75–77, 191–92, 214–15.

week), and, hence, have sex only a fraction of the time they think about it,[34] whereas, statistically, wives think about sex slightly more frequently than they have sex—on average, about two times per week. This gender disparity is largely explained by differing levels of testosterone, men having on average ten to twenty times more testosterone than women.

2. WE DIFFER IN WHAT WE WANT FROM AND ENJOY ABOUT SEX.

When women were asked what they most liked about sex, the overwhelming majority answered "physical and/or emotional closeness" even over orgasm. This corresponds with the famous survey by Ann Landers, who asked her female readers, "Would you be content to be held close and treated tenderly and forget about 'the act' [sexual intercourse]?" A whopping 72 percent of the one hundred thousand women who responded to Landers's survey answered "yes."[35] The overwhelming majority of men, however, find the pleasure and release of orgasm to be the most enjoyable aspect of sex. This gender disparity is largely explained in terms of male/female anatomical differences; males alone have a buildup of semen.

3. WE DIFFER IN WHAT WE NEED FOR MAXIMUM SEXUAL AROUSAL AND ORGASM.

On average, women need more time to build peak sexual arousal than men do. Thirty to forty-five minutes is "the optimum duration of lovemaking for a high level of sexual satisfaction" for most women.[36] Very few men need this much time for maximum arousal and orgasm. Furthermore, unlike men, most women—as many as two out of three— cannot achieve orgasm by intercourse alone. They often need additional manual or oral stimulation. This difference is explained anatomically. The clitoris has roughly the same number of pleasure receptors as does the penis, but it is located several inches from the vaginal opening. Thus, a woman's clitoris does not receive the kind of direct, intense stimulation from intercourse that a man's penis does.

34. Shanor, *The Shanor Study*. Shanor found that males ages twelve to nineteen think about sex twenty times an hour.

35. "What 100,000 Women Told Ann Landers," *Reader's Digest*, August 1985, 44–46, cited in Hart, Weber, and Taylor, *Secrets of Eve*, 253.

36. Hart, Weber, and Taylor, *Secrets of Eve*, 168.

4. WE DIFFER IN OUR ENERGY RESOURCES FOR SEX.

The vast majority of Christian women surveyed value and desire sexual relations with their spouse (only 4 percent said they had no sexual desire), but often lack the energy. In particular, 55 percent of women with children at home and 44 percent of women in their early to mid forties indicated they lacked the energy for sex. While lack of energy for sex also affects men, this is much less common. For many men, sex provides relief and tranquility when they are exhausted.

5. WE DIFFER IN OUR CONCERNS ABOUT BODY IMAGE.

This was one of the more dramatic findings of the survey of Christian women. Two-thirds of those surveyed said they were negatively affected sexually by one or more aspects of body image. The menstrual cycle was a particularly significant factor negatively impacting body image and sexuality; 39 percent of the women reported this. Again, body image can negatively impact male sexuality, but this is much less common.[37]

6. WE DIFFER IN HOW OFTEN WE WANT TO HAVE SEX.

Generally speaking, men want to have sex considerably more often than women do. In the *Secrets of Eve* study, only 40 percent of the wives said they wanted sex more often, but 70 percent reported their husbands wanted sex more often. Interestingly, while men's most common sexual complaint related to frequency of sex, one of women's most common frustrations was duration of sex.[38]

7. WE DIFFER IN HOW WE CONNECT SEXUALLY.

"[M]en and women connect differently. Women first want to talk and feel close and then (if the time is right) have sex. Men frequently use sex as a means of achieving closeness."[39] This sexual difference can create great frustration for a husband who wants to have sex in order to

---

37. One recent closely related research study of fifty-three couples highlights male/female differences in this area. Researchers found that wives' perceptions of their sexual attractiveness accounted for 6 percent of the variance in husbands' marital satisfaction, but it accounted for 19 percent of the variance in wives' marital satisfaction (after controlling for wives' body mass index, global self-esteem, and neuroticism); Meltzer and McNulty, "Body Image and Marital Satisfaction."

38. Hart, Weber, and Taylor, *Secrets of Eve*, 164.

39. Ibid., 257.

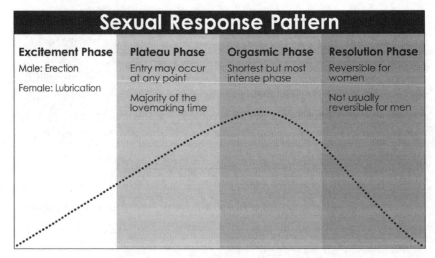

FIGURE 1: Sexual Response Pattern[40]

feel a sense of emotional bondedness to his wife, while she needs to feel bonded to him in order to feel ready for sex.[41]

Patterns of Sexual Response

In order to understand the intricate details of men's and women's sexual responses, let us look at the four phases defined by Masters and Johnson: excitement; plateau; orgasm; and resolution.[42] Sexual desire is the emotional prelude to this four-phase sequence.

The excitement phase is our initial sexual arousal, reflected for the man in an erection and for the woman in vaginal lubrication. The plateau is the longest phase of lovemaking, and, during this time, arousal intensifies in preparation for the sexual release. The orgasmic phase is the briefest and most intense phase, culminating in the sexual release itself. Finally, the resolution phase is when the body returns to its unaroused state. It is important to note that there are diverse individual differences in feeling, intensity, and timing within this four-phase sequence.

40. Penner, *The Gift of Sex*, 71.

41. It is important to note that the authors of this study emphasize that these differences reflect the good creation of God. They do not reflect deficiencies in either gender. Thus, these findings can provide important insights for understanding and appreciating one's spouse.

42. Masters and Johnson, *Human Sexual Response*, 3–8.

Doug Rosenau sensitively addresses the differing levels of involvement that exist in lovemaking. He notes that it is critically important for a wife to give herself permission to say "no" so that she can say "yes" to varying levels of involvement in lovemaking.[43] Duty or pity sex is often offered out of guilt or obligation and is typically never enjoyed by either partner. Rosenau develops a continuum of sexual involvement from duty to passionate responding that we have found helpful.[44] We have adapted his continuum in figure 2 below. Many women describe nurturing sex as an aspect of their receptive desire for their husband. Wise partners take responsibility for the nurturing of their own sexual desire toward their spouse. This desire is best motivated out of love for the other and communicated in respectful but clear ways.

Assertive Desire .... Receptive Desire
Passionate Sex .... Nurturing Sex .... Duty Sex

FIGURE 2: Levels of personal involvement in lovemaking continuum

In summary, a couple's task in lovemaking is to develop a mutually enjoyable style of intercourse, manual/oral stimulation, dreams, fantasies, visual input, kissing, caressing, hugging, and talking, which are prioritized, private, and sacred to their relationship. As a clinician, I (Celestia) have found that when I focus a couple on intensifying the first nine stages of bonding, the final stages of sexual expression begin to take care of themselves. In other words, for most couples, by the time they move through the first nine stages of bonding, I typically don't need to see them again!

WHAT HAPPENS FOR WOMEN?

A woman, in general, needs more energy for sex than a man does, because her mind and body are not physiologically connected as they are for him. To make matters more complicated, her sexual desire is not static, but is in a constant state of flux, dependent upon monthly biological rhythms tied to her body's reproductive design. At times, she may experience (physiological) genital arousal while not feeling emotionally

43. Rosenau, *A Celebration of Sex,* 168–69.
44. Ibid., 169.

aroused.[45] In fact, her mind could be creating a grocery list during sex if she is not properly attuned and intentionally focused. Her biological rhythms create ever-shifting needs around touch, emotion, and environment. How can any man know how to navigate all of this without her assistance? What is a couple to do?!

For these reasons, the most important response a wife can have is to express her needs assertively and the nature of her sexual desire for her husband. She must remember that her sexual needs and desires will not always match his, so her boldness in coaching and directing him is necessary. He will find this both helpful and attractive!

Her sexual needs include the following, illustrated by couples we have counseled:

- *To be pursued sexually by her husband.* "Sex is very important to me. It makes me feel close to my husband. When he doesn't pursue me sexually, I feel inadequate and profoundly rejected. I don't feel beautiful."

- *To please her husband.* "My husband has a hard time understanding that often my greatest enjoyment in sex is getting to be the one who meets his sexual needs. I love to bring him pleasure in this way. That for me is better than an orgasm any day!"

- *Spending time together.* "I just love it when my husband walks with me at night."

- *Time to talk every day.* "If we do not have time to talk and connect during the day, it is difficult for me to even think about making love at night."

- *Romance.* "I love it when my husband does those little things that make me feel important to him."

- *To be able to say "no."* "I need to know that when I am too tired, or feeling disconnected and unable to make love, that my husband is gentle and responds with patience. That makes me feel very loved."

- *To be appreciated for more than sex.* "I hate it when my husband only touches me in sexual ways or when he wants sex. It makes me feel used and cheap, like his release valve!" "I need him to touch and

45. Chivers et al., "Agreement."

caress me at those times when he knows that we will not be having sex. This makes me feel so loved."

WHAT HAPPENS FOR MEN?

Most men want intimacy, and this can be misplaced or miscommunicated in their drive for sexual experience. However, he wants more from sex than the physiological release he receives from the act itself. *He wants the same soul intimacy that she desires,* though he typically has difficulty expressing this. He often feels chronically misunderstood and judged by women in his life. It is easy for his wife to make assumptions about his desires and needs based on the sexual distortions of her past and the sexualized culture around them. He receives cultural messages daily telling him that he cannot be weak, sensitive, or have relational needs. This has probably been reinforced for him by messages from his past by fathers, uncles, or coaches. "Boys who cry are sissies!" "Man up and take it!" She needs to know and share in these stories so that she can better understand and love him. She needs to be increasingly sensitized to his vulnerabilities and deepest fears—that he isn't man enough or that he simply isn't enough, period.

His sexual needs include the following, again illustrated by couples we have counseled:[46]

- *A more complete sexual experience—a soul connection.* "During puberty, most of us either get good information, bad information, or no information. I realize now [a sixty-five-year-old husband] that my historically insatiable desire for sex was really a cry for intimacy."

- *Frequent sex.* "My wife will never understand my sexual needs! It's embarrassing to say this, but my self-confidence is tied to our time together."

- *To be listened to—help in baring his soul.* "I have seen a female counselor for the past year. In many ways, she has felt like the patient, nurturing mother I never had. For the first time, I am learning about the complexities of a woman's sexuality and my real needs as a man, and I have been married for thirty years!"

46. See Hart, *The Sexual Man,* 76–81.

- *For his sexuality to be respected.* "I have never felt understood by a woman—not my mom, not my sister, and now not by my wife. She demeans my need for sex and makes me feel like a pervert!"

- *To please his wife.* "My wife does not understand how disappointing it is to me when she doesn't enjoy our time together sexually. I want that more than anything!"

The artful wife will draw out her husband by asking sensitive questions in a safe environment to better understand him. What does making love mean to him after all? When she enjoys and receives his body into her own, what does that communicate to his soul? What does he feel when she *loves* making love to him? Invite him to speak, to write, to share. Coach him in articulating his heart. When women can better understand male sexuality, they are far more motivated to prioritize lovemaking within their marriage; what an exquisite gift this is to their husbands!

Exercises and Questions for Reflection and Sharing: Hand to Genitals

1. Read together the poetry of Song of Solomon in 7:12–14. Practice daily, direct declarations of love for each other until they are natural expressions.

2. What are the sexual gender differences that are most impacting you as a couple? How does your spouse best meet your sexual needs? What are you most thankful for?

3. Are there any changes you would like to make sexually? Are your sexual needs being met at the present time? Explain.

4. Is there anything you need to disclose or confess that you have been convicted of after reading this chapter? If so, do it now.

5. After reading the discussion on the biblical parameters of sexual expression, are there any changes either one of you needs to make in your lovemaking? What is the one thing you most want your spouse to understand about your sexual needs?

6. Are you sexually protected as a man? As a woman? As a couple? If not, what immediate changes need to be made? Commit to them now.

7. Take some time during the next twenty-four hours and write a love letter to your spouse. Describe what making love means to you as a man, as a woman. Describe how you are impacted by your sexual intimacy as a couple—what are you trying to communicate when you make love to your spouse?

8. Close this time by praying for each other and for protection for your sexual relationship. Include confession, repentance, and forgiveness as necessary.

Stage Twelve: Genital to Genital

How beautiful you are, my darling! Oh, how beautiful!
Your eyes are doves.
How handsome you are, my lover! Oh, how charming!
And our bed is verdant.

—Song 1:15–16 (NIV)

Protect your relationship by protecting your sex life. What will be your frequency of lovemaking? There is surprising consistency in the intimacy research, which is congruent with our experience. As a clinician, I (Celestia) have been conducting informal "armchair research" for years by asking husbands within the context of marital counseling about the frequency of sexual intimacy they need in order to maintain an emotional connection to their wives. With surprising consistency, they have responded with either "approximately every three days or so" or "a couple of times a week." We have found this to be a helpful general guide for marriage. For instance, if we as a couple are too stressed, too tired, or too conflicted to make love every three or four days, we are probably too busy. We must take individual responsibility for this prioritization as an expression of our love for each other. Sex is a whole lot more fun when we work at it.

The Act of Surrender

Sexual play and stimulation typically and eventually lead to entry—his penis into her vagina. Entry is most desired and successful when there is proper vaginal lubrication for her and an erect penis for him; his readiness is external while hers is internal. This helps to explain why some women report being unsure of reaching orgasm. Most men cannot relate to this uncertainty. An orgasm is

> a reflex response that is triggered when there is enough buildup of sexual tension from effective stimulation and the freedom to pursue it without inhibition or fear of being out of control. Arousal builds to intensity, causing engorgement or a building of sexual tension felt throughout the whole body, yet most specifically in the genitals. This engorgement triggers the reflex of the orgasm.[47]

It is important to remember that the physical signs of readiness do not always ensure her emotional readiness. In the New Testament, all the primary passages that give instructions to husbands, wives, and households include an affirmation of equality and mutuality, often at the beginning or end of each section.[48] Not only are husbands and wives equal in God's sight, but they also have mutual rights and responsibilities to each other. By God's design, she is the only one who can know and thus signal her physical and emotional readiness. *Entry by him is done by invitation only.*[49] Her needs must be clearly communicated and respected because it is her body that is being entered. She will be more relaxed at this stage of lovemaking if she is the one to signal readiness. Her signal can be verbal or nonverbal, by holding and moving his penis toward her vagina, through thrusting her pelvis, or more subtly through moans. Because her body generally requires longer for readiness than his, she will need to feel loved, trusting in his patience and gentleness during this stage.

47. Penner, *The Gift of Sex*, 156–57.

48. 1 Cor 7:2–5; Eph 5:21; Col 4:1; 1 Pet 3:7. Equality and mutuality is not explicit in the Colossian household code, as it is in the other three passages, but it is implicit in the way Paul threads and unites the commands given to the various household members to their united, supreme Lord, Jesus Christ.

49. The authors would like to express gratitude to the Sexual Wholeness Institute and to other Christian theologians and clinicians who stress the importance of mutuality within the whole of marriage, but especially within the sex act itself.

Not only are there gender differences for couples, there are wildly divergent individual differences in sexual desire, arousal patterns, and continuums of comfort as well. Develop and expand your language of love, talk openly about your sexual needs without shame or embarrassment. Talk during sex, after sex, about sex. Develop nonverbal signals that indicate your desire for sexual activity—a candle lit, a particular nightgown, a passionate kiss, nibbles on the ear. Communicate your pleasure and enjoyment in each other's bodies. Be passionate and unashamed in your expressions of delight. *These are your benedictions of love.*

As we write this section, we are reminded of the many ways "making love" differs from sex as an act separate from relationship. In one-night stands or pornography, the consumers of sex must emotionally numb, or "check out," in order to focus on their own intense sexual release. In that sense, pornography objectifies both men and women, the consumers and the women "consumed." In beautiful contrast, marital sexual love is the spiritual experience of an inner touching of another, an awareness of being present and connected with another, the recognition of someone and something outside of our own bodies which anchors us, not only to each other, but to God himself. Instead of dictating terms of control, a husband surrenders his physical and sexual self into her hands—trusting her as his guide. Waiting for her invitation, her readiness, he does not demand sexual acts of her, but instead relinquishes control, allowing her space enough to offer her body to him freely as a sacred gift of love, given over and over again.

Read aloud Ephesians 5:21–33 and meditate on the biblical symbolism. During marital lovemaking, he is being invited into the inner sanctuary of her body. He is offering himself to her, just as Christ offers himself to us. Christ is ready and desirous of entering our lives, loving and guiding us in ways that he knows will bring us life. However, he gives us the choice to receive or reject his invitations of presence and life. He doesn't force his way in. He waits for our readiness and invitation. He teaches us to trust him through his faithful love of us; he longs to penetrate us with his love. He loves us first and in ways that cast out fear, alluring us into a love relationship with himself.[50]

50. Hosea 2.

Exercises and Questions for Reflection and Sharing: Genital to Genital

1. Read aloud Song of Solomon 1:15–17, which is a poem depicting sexual love enjoyed outdoors. Then read Ephesians 5:21–33. Talk about these passages and the implications for your sexual intimacy.

2. Create a mission statement for the sexual expression of bonding within your marriage. Wrap the twelve stages of bonding into this mission statement as you desire. Customize the expression, the declarations, and the purpose of sexuality within your marriage. Make it specific and clear. Print it, post it, and read it often. Let it be the compass that protects and navigates you through the years ahead. Your sexuality is God's most magnificent gift to you as a couple. Protect it. Celebrate it. Develop it. Enjoy it. For, by it, you will be creating and shaping your love over and over again!

CONCLUSION

Craft, maintain, and protect this beautiful gift of sex. It holds much of the mystery to the bond between the two of you. Touch often, caress often, kiss often, and make love as often as you can. As the years steal the beauty from your body, you will be declared beautiful again and again through this sacred act of marriage. Touch and be touched. Laugh. Celebrate. Worship.

APPENDIX A

Married Couples' Emotional Intimacy Quotient

	True	False
I often feel anxious when my partner is angry.		
My partner seldom shares with me his/her disappointments.		
It's easy for me to read my partner's feelings when we talk. If not, why?		
My partner seldom makes eye contact with me.		
I'm often surprised by my partner's expressed feelings.		
I generally feel the freedom to talk openly with my partner about my feelings.		
No matter how frustrated I get, I keep talking until we achieve resolution. If not, describe why:		
It's enjoyable for me to share with my partner about my day. If not, why?		
I can identify the three most disappointing events in my partner's childhood.		
I often blow up at my partner.		
I never feel angry or frustrated.		
It's easy for me to know what I feel.		
I can identify a significant fear and have already shared this with my partner.		
I don't feel that I have a voice with my partner.		
I often feel lonely.		
I often use humor or sarcasm to communicate.		
I always feel guilty when I get angry or frustrated.		

	True	False
My partner desires to know my true feelings, even when they will be painful to hear.		
I often feel agitated.		
My partner would say that I understand his/her insecurities and factor that into our relationship.		

Note: the higher your total score, the deeper level of emotional intimacy you are experiencing in this relationship.

Score as follows:

One point for every "true" response on items
3, 6, 7, 8, 9, 12, 13, 18, 20 =   ____

One point for every "false" response on items
1, 2, 4, 5, 10, 11, 14, 15, 16, 17, 19 =   ____

Total points = ____

Appendix B

Singles' Emotional Intimacy Quotient

	True	False
I often feel anxious when my best friend is angry.		
My best friend seldom shares with me his/her disappointments.		
It's easy for me to read my best friend's feelings when we talk. If not, why?		
My best friend seldom makes eye contact with me.		
I'm often surprised by my best friend's expressed feelings.		
I generally feel the freedom to talk openly with my best friend about my feelings.		
No matter how frustrated I get, I keep talking until we achieve resolution. If not, describe why:		
It's enjoyable for me to share with my best friend about my day. If not, why?		
I can identify the three most disappointing events in my best friend's childhood.		
I often blow up at my best friend.		
I never feel angry or frustrated.		
It's easy for me to know what I feel.		
I can identify a significant fear and have already shared this with my best friend.		
I don't feel that I have a voice with my best friend.		
I often feel lonely.		

	True	False
I often use humor or sarcasm to communicate.		
I always feel guilty when I get angry or frustrated.		
My best friend desires to know my true feelings, even when they will be painful to hear.		
I often feel agitated.		
My best friend would say that I understand his/her insecurities and factor that into our relationship.		

Note: the higher your total score, the deeper level of emotional intimacy you are experiencing in this relationship.

Score as follows:

One point for every "true" response on items
3, 6, 7, 8, 9, 12, 13, 18, 20 = ____

One point for every "false" response on items
1, 2, 4, 5, 10, 11, 14, 15, 16, 17, 19 = ____

Total points = ____

Appendix C

Married Couples' Relational Intimacy Quotient

		True	False
1.	I know my partner's favorite color.		
2.	I know what section of the newspaper my partner is likely to read first.		
3.	I can describe, in moderate detail, the home environment in which my partner was raised.		
4.	I know what makes my partner laugh.		
5.	I know my partner's favorite music and why he/she prefers it.		
6.	I know my partner's dreams for the future.		
7.	I know my partner's three most significant childhood events.		
8.	I know how my partner's parents would describe him/her.		
9.	I can identify two of the happiest times in my partner's life.		
10.	I know my partner's greatest loss in life.		
11.	I can name my partner's two best friends.		
12.	I can describe a decision my partner made before we met that my partner now regrets.		
13.	I know my partner's dream vacation destination.		
14.	I know my partner's deepest insecurity.		
15.	I know my partner's physical characteristic he/she is most unhappy about.		
16.	I can identify, in specific detail, three dreams my partner has experienced in the past six months.		
17.	I know what is most challenging for my partner during a typical workday.		
18.	I can name two of my partner's childhood friends.		
19.	I can describe my partner's religious beliefs.		
20.	I can identify and describe my partner's favorite memory of one of our most intimate times together.		

Note: the higher your total score, the deeper level of relational intimacy you are experiencing in this relationship.

Score as follows:

One point for every "true" response on items 1–20 =   ____

Total points = ____

Appendix D

Singles' Relational Intimacy Quotient

	True	False
I spend at least seven hours a week with my friends (outside of work).		
My friends would say I take criticism well.		
When I am feeling insecure, I pull away from people.		
I avoid deep conversation in my significant relationships		
To be quite honest, I don't need people.		
When I have something uncomfortable to say, I use email.		
I have deep struggles that I do not share.		
In my significant relationships, it is difficult for me to communicate my needs.		
I am often silent when I really disagree.		
I don't confront. It is easier to "keep the peace."		
I feel more attached to my pet than I do to anyone else.		
Text messaging is man's best invention for relationships.		
My friends have no idea how frustrated they make me.		
I spend ten or more hours a week watching television or movies		
I can identify the three most significant events in my closest friend's life.		
I feel deeply understood by my closest friends.		
I feel I never really measure up to others' expectations.		
I can identify three major struggles for my closest friend and have taken specific steps to support him/her with these struggles.		
I have terminated relationships through the Internet.		
It is difficult for me to know how to have close relationships with the opposite sex without being sexual.		

Note: the higher your total score, the deeper level of relational intimacy you are experiencing in your relationships.

Score as follows:

One point for every "true" response on items
1, 2, 15, 16, 18 =   ____

One point for every "false" response on items
3, 4, 5, 6, 7, 8, 9, 10, 11, 12, 13, 14, 17, 19, 20 =   ____

Total points = ____

Appendix E

Married Couples' Physical (Nonerotic) Intimacy Quotient

		True	False
1.	I often desire more affection from my partner.		
2.	It's natural for me to say "I love you."		
3.	My partner sometimes touches me in ways that make me feel uncomfortable. Give an example:		
4.	My partner only kisses me when he/she wants to have sex.		
5.	We often hold hands.		
6.	Touching my partner makes me feel uncomfortable.		
7.	I believe that changing my physical appearance would alter my partner's love for me.		
8.	I am uncomfortable or embarrassed to undress in front of my partner. Why?		
9.	My partner enjoys giving and or receiving backrubs.		
10.	My partner often touches my face.		
11.	I am most able to sleep while touching my partner.		
12.	My partner enjoys my touch.		
13.	In a typical day, apart from sex, my partner and I kiss a minimum of five times.		
14.	It's typical for my partner to touch me in playful ways that make me feel good.		
15.	My confidence as a man or woman has grown significantly because of the affection he/she has offered me.		
16.	My partner knows what characteristic of his/her face I enjoy the most.		

		True	False
17.	I fantasize about my partner.		
18.	I'm critical of my partner's physical flaws.		
19.	My partner and I have three or more rituals of touching affectionately (example of kissing after prayer or hugging goodbye).		
20.	Our affection has diminished the longer we have been married.		

Note: the higher your total score, the deeper level of (nonerotic) physical intimacy you are experiencing in this relationship.

Score as follows:

One point for every "true" response on items
2, 5, 9, 10, 11, 12, 13, 14, 15, 16, 17, 19 = ____

One point for every "false" response on items
1, 3, 4, 6, 7, 8, 18, 20 = ____

Total points = ____

APPENDIX F

Married Couples' Sexual Intimacy Quotient

		True	False
1.	I have never experienced an orgasm with my partner.		
2.	My partner enjoys stimulating me in foreplay.		
3.	We seldom kiss during sex.		
4.	I enjoy being stimulated during foreplay.		
5.	After sex with my partner, I feel dirty.		
6.	I enjoy looking at my partner's face during sex.		
7.	I feel closer to my partner after sex.		
8.	My partner often uses sex or withholds sex as punishment or manipulation.		
9.	I sometimes feel coerced to have sex with my partner.		
10.	We frequently go two weeks or longer without sex.		
11.	My partner and I are unable to talk about our sex life comfortably.		
12.	I know and feel comfortable with what my partner wants in our sex life and offer it.		
13.	My partner sometimes asks me to perform sexually in ways that make me uncomfortable.		
14.	It is difficult for me to say "no" to my partner sexually.		
15.	I strategize to prioritize our sex life in our marriage.		
16.	Our sex life has increased my confidence in being a man or a woman.		
17.	I sometimes have difficulty focusing on my partner when we have sex.		
18.	I still feel guilt about my sex life before meeting my partner.		
19.	My partner and I have discussed and reached resolution on any premarital sexual involvement with each other.		
20.	My partner or I periodically look at pornography.		
21.	I masturbate once a week.		

		True	False
22.	I worry about my partner having an affair.		
23.	I often fantasize about having an affair.		
24.	There are portions of my sexual history that I conceal from my spouse.		
25.	My partner and I sometimes watch R- or X-rated movies to "spice up" our sex life.		

Note: the higher your total score, the deeper level of sexual intimacy you are experiencing in this relationship.

Score as follows:

One point for every "true" response on items
2, 4, 6, 7, 12, 15, 16, 19 =   ____

One point for every "false" response on items
1, 3, 5, 8, 9, 10, 11, 13, 14, 17, 18, 20, 21, 22, 23, 24, 25 =   ____

Total points = ____

APPENDIX G

Singles' Sexual Health Quotient

	True	False
I am comfortable giving and receiving affectionate (nonerotic) touch with family and close friends.		
I have looked at pornography in the last three months.		
I have memories that I have not shared with anyone I trust of being touched in ways that made me feel uncomfortable as a child.		
I like being a man/woman.		
I have memories from my junior high and/or high school years that still trigger shame.		
Self-disclosure is difficult for me in my significant relationships.		
I have at least two people in my life who know and love the real me. I can tell them anything.		
I have secrets about my sexual past that I have not shared with anyone I trust.		
The closer I get to someone, the more anxiety I feel.		
As a man, I frequently fantasize in a way that sexualizes women. As a woman, I spend more time fantasizing about relationships with men than actually experiencing relationships with men.		
As a man, I like the company of women. As a woman I like the company of men.		
I often feel inadequate as a man/woman.		
When I see a nude reflection of myself in the mirror, I feel shame or embarrassment.		
I struggle with same-sex attraction.		
I believe that changing my physical appearance would deepen my sense of value/worth.		
I struggle with compulsive masturbation.		

	True	False
Sex has dirty connotations to me.		
My unmet sexual/emotional longings drive me to a deeper intimacy with Christ.		
I have difficulty setting sexual boundaries with others.		
I am not embarrassed to be single.		

Note: the higher your total score, the deeper level of sexual health you are experiencing.

Score as follows:

One point for every "true" response on items
1, 4, 7, 11, 18, 20 =   ____

One point for every "false" response on items
2, 3, 5, 6, 8, 9, 10, 12, 13, 14, 15, 16, 17, 19 =   ____

Total points = ____

Bibliography

Allender, Dan B., and Tremper R. Longman. *Intimate Allies*. Wheaton, IL: Tyndale, 1995.

Barclay, John. *Obeying the Truth: A Study of Paul's Ethics in Galatians*. Edinburgh: T. & T. Clark, 1988.

Barger, Lilian Calles. *Eve's Revenge: Women and a Spirituality of the Body*. Grand Rapids: Brazos, 2003.

Barron, Martin, and Michael Kimmel. "Sexual Violence in Three Pornographic Media: Toward a Sociological Explanation." *The Journal of Sex Research* 37 (2000): 161–68.

Bartels, A., and S. Zeki. "The Neural Basis of Romantic Love." *NeuroReport* 11 (2000): 3829–34.

Barth, Karl. *Church Dogmatics*. Edinburgh: T. & T. Clark, 1958.

Beauchaine, Theodore P., et al. "Multifinality in the Development of Personality Disorders: A Biology × Sex × Environment Interaction Model of Antisocial and Borderline Traits." *Development & Psychopathology* 21 (2009): 735–70.

Bergner, Raymond M., and Ana J. Bridges. "The Significance of Heavy Pornography Involvement for Romantic Partners: Research and Clinical Implications." *Journal of Sex & Marital Therapy* 28 (2002): 193–206.

Bloesch, Donald. *God the Almighty*. Downers Grove, IL: InterVarsity, 1995.

Bolen, R. M., and M. Scannapieco. "Prevalence of Child Sexual Abuse: A Corrective Metanalysis." *Social Service Review* 73 (1999): 281–313.

Brizendine, Louann. *The Female Brain*. New York: Morgan Road Books, 2006.

———. *The Male Brain*. New York: Broadway Books, 2010.

Buechner, Frederick. *Listening to Your Life: Daily Meditations with Frederick Buechner*. New York: HarperCollins, 1992.

———. *The Magnificent Defeat*. San Francisco: Harper & Row, 1985.

———. *Telling Secrets*. New York: HarperCollins, 1991.

Bush, Elizabeth. "The Use of Human Touch to Improve the Well-Being of Older Adults." *Journal of Holistic Nursing* 19 (2001): 256–70.

Carter, C. S. "Oxytocin and Sexual Behaviour." *Neuroscience and Biobehavioural Reviews* 16 (1992): 131–44.

Carter, C. S., A. C. DeVries, and L. L. Getz. "Physiological Substrates of Mammalian Monogamy: The Prairie Vole Model." *Neuroscience and Biobehavioural Reviews* 19 (1995): 39–45.

Cassileth, B. R., and A. J. Vickers. "Massage Therapy for Symptom Control: Outcome Study at a Major Cancer Center." *Journal of Pain and Symptom Management* 28 (2004): 244–49.

Chandler, Joan, et al. "Living Alone: Its Place in Household Formation and Change." *Sociological Research Online* 9 (2004). http://www.socresonline.org.uk/9/3/chandler.html.

Chivers, Meredith L., et al. "Agreement of Self-Reported and Genital Measures of Sexual Arousal in Men and Women: A Meta-Analysis." *Archives of Sexual Behavior* 39 (2010): 5–56.

Christensen, Sherie A., and Richard B. Miller. "Areas of Desired Change among Married Midlife Individuals." *Journal of Couple and Relationship Therapy* 5 (2006): 35–57.

Chugani, Harry T., et al. "Local Brain Functional Activity Following Early Deprivation: A Study of Postinstitutionalized Romanian Orphans." *NeuroImage* 14 (2001): 1290–1301.

Clines, D. J. A. "The Image of God in Man." *Tyndale Bulletin* 19 (1968): 62–69.

Connellan, J., S. et al. "Sex Differences in Human Neonatal Social Perception." *Infant Behavior and Development* 23 (2001): 113–18.

Cozolino, Louis. *The Neuroscience of Human Relationships: Attachment and the Developing Brain.* New York: W. W. Norton, 2006.

———. *The Neuroscience of Psychotherapy: Building and Rebuilding the Human Brain.* New York: W. W. Norton, 2002.

Crary, David. "Study—College Students More Narcissistic." *Boston Globe*, Feb. 27, 2007, http://www.boston.com/news/education/higher/articles/2007/02/27/study_college_students_more_narcissistic.

Danker, Frederick William, ed. *A Greek-English Lexicon of the New Testament and Other Early Christian Literature*, 3rd ed. Chicago: University of Chicago Press, 2000.

Davidson, Richard M. *Flame of Yahweh: Sexuality in the Old Testament.* Peabody, Mass.: Hendrickson, 2007.

De Bellis, Michael D. "The Psychobiology of Neglect." *Child Maltreatment* 10 (2005): 150–72.

Dworkin, Andrea. *Pornography: Men Possessing Women.* Rev. ed. New York: Plume, 1989.

Eigengerg, Helen M. *Women Battering in the United States: Till Death Do Us Part.* Prospect Heights, IL: Waveland Press, 2001.

Field, Tiffany. "American Adolescents Touch Each Other Less and Are More Aggressive toward Their Peers as Compared with French Adolescents." *Adolescence* 34 (1999): 753–58.

———. "Preschoolers in America are Touched Less and Are More Aggressive than Preschoolers in France." *Early Child Development and Care* 151 (1999): 11–17.

———. *Touch.* Cambridge, Mass: MIT Press, 2001.

Field, Tiffany, et al. "Behavior State Matching during Interactions of Preadolescent Friends Versus Acquaintances." *Developmental Psychology* 28 (1992): 242–50.

———. "Tactile/kinesthetic Stimulation Effects on Preterm Neonates." *Pediatrics* 77 (1986): 654–58.

Fisher, Helen. *Why We Love: The Nature and Chemistry of Romantic Love.* New York: Owl Books, 2004.

Fisher, J. A., and S. J. Gallant. "Effects of Touch on Hospitalized Patients." In *Advances in Touch,* edited by N. Gunzenhauser et al., 141–47. Skillman, NJ: Johnson & Johnson, 1990.

Fisher, L., et al. "Problems Reported by Parents of Romanian Orphans Adopted to British Columbia." *International Journal of Behavioral Development* 20 (1997): 67–82.

Gaither, Mark W. *Redemptive Divorce: A Biblical Process that Offers Guidance for the Suffering Partner, Healing for the Offending Spouse, and the Best Catalyst for Restoration.* Nashville: Thomas Nelson, 2008.

Gardner, Christian J. "Tangled in the Worst of the Web." *Christianity Today* 45:4 (March 5, 2001): 42–49.

Gossai, Hemchand. "Divine Evaluation and the Quest for a Suitable Companionship." *Cross Currents* 52 (2003): 543–52.

Gottman, John. *Why Marriages Succeed or Fail . . . and How You Can Make Yours Last.* New York: Simon & Schuster, 1994.

Grenz, Stanley J. *Sexual Ethics: An Evangelical Perspective.* Rev. ed. Louisville, KY: Westminster John Knox, 1997.

———. *The Social God and the Relational Self: A Trinitarian Theology of the Imago Dei.* Louisville: Westminster John Knox, 2001.

———. "Theological Foundations for Male-Female Relationships." *Journal of the Evangelical Theological Society* 41 (1998): 615–30.

———. *Theology for the Community of God.* Nashville: Broadman & Holman, 1994.

Gushee, David P. *Only Human: Christian Reflections on the Journey toward Wholeness.* San Francisco: Jossey-Bass, 2005.

Alan Guttmacher Institute. "Teen Sex and Pregnancy." http://www.guttmacher.org/pubs/fb_teen_sex.pdf.

Hall, Laurie. *An Affair of the Mind.* Wheaton, IL: Tyndale, 1996.

Hamilton, Victor P. *The Book of Genesis Chapters 1–17.* Grand Rapids: Eerdmans, 1990.

Harley, Willard F. *His Needs, Her Needs: Building an Affair-Proof Marriage.* Old Tappan, NJ: Revell, 1986.

Hart, Archibald D. *The Sexual Man.* Dallas: Word, 1994.

Hart, Archibald D., Catherine Hart Weber, and Debra L. Taylor. *Secrets of Eve: Understanding the Mystery of Female Sexuality.* Nashville: Word, 1998.

Hasel, Gerhard. "The Meaning of 'Let Us' in Gn 1:26." *Andrews University Seminary Studies* 13 (1975): 58–66.

Hiller, Janice. "Speculations on the Links between Feelings, Emotions, and Sexual Behaviour: Are Vasopressin and Oxytocin Involved?" *Sexual & Relationship Therapy* 19 (2004): 393–412.

Hoekema, Anthony A. *Created in God's Image.* Grand Rapids: Eerdmans, 1986.

Hsiu-Chen, Yeh, et al. "Relationships among Sexual Satisfaction, Marital Quality, and Marital Instability at Midlife." *Journal of Family Psychology* 20 (2006): 339–43.

Hugenberger, Gordon. *Marriage as a Covenant.* Leiden: Brill, 1994.

Hybels, Bill, and Rob Wilkins. *Tender Love: God's Gift of Sexual Intimacy.* Chicago: Moody, 1993.

Instone-Brewer, David. *Divorce and Remarriage in the Bible: The Social and Literary Context.* Grand Rapids: Eerdmans, 2002.

Ironson, G., et al. "Massage Therapy Is Associated with Enhancement of the Immune System's Cytotoxic Capacity." *International Journal of Neuroscience* 84 (1996): 205–17.

Jensen, Robert. "Cruel to be Hard: Men and Pornography." *Sexual Assault Report,* January/February 2004, 33–34, 47–48.

———. *Getting Off: Pornography and the End of Masculinity.* Cambridge, Mass.: South End Press, 2007.

Jensen, Robert, Gail Dines, and Ann Russo. *Pornography: The Production and Consumption of Inequality.* New York: Routledge, 1998.

Johnson, Rebecca, Kevin Browne, and Catherine Hamilton-Giachritsis. "Young Children in Institutional Care at Risk of Harm." *Trauma, Violence, & Abuse* 7 (2006): 34–60.

Johnson, Steven. "Emotions and the Brain: Love." *Discover*, May 2003. http://discover magazine.com/2003/may/featlove.

———. *Mind Wide Open: Your Brain and the Neuroscience of Everyday Life*. New York: Scribner, 2004.

Jong, Erica. "Scenes from an Open Marriage." *ELLE Magazine*, April 2006. http://www .ericajong.com/articles/ElleMagazine.pdf.

Jong-Fast, Molly. *Girl [Maladjusted]: True Stories from a Semi-Celebrity Childhood*. New York: Villard, 2006.

Jourard, S. M. "An Exploratory Study of Body Accessibility." *British Journal of Social Change and Clinical* Psychology 5 (1966): 221–31.

Joy, Donald. *Bonding: Relationships in the Image of God*. Waco, TX: Word, 1985.

Kaler, Sandra, and B. J. Freeman. "Analysis of Environmental Deprivation: Cognitive and Social Development in Romanian Orphans." *Journal of Child Psychology and Psychiatry* 35 (1994): 769–81.

Karen, Robert. *Becoming Attached: First Relationships and How they Shape Our Capacity to Love*. New York: Oxford University Press, 1998.

Keenan, James F. *Ethics of the Word: Voices in the Catholic Church Today*. Lanham, MD: Rowman & Littlefield, 2010.

Kinney, Mary Ellen, et al. "Therapeutic Massage and Healing Touch Improve Symptoms in Cancer." *Integrative Cancer Therapies* 2 (2003): 332–44.

Kosfeld, Michael, et al. "Oxytocin Increases Trust in Humans." *Nature* 435 (2 June 2005): 673–76.

Kreeft, Peter. "Is There Sex in Heaven?" http://www.peterkreeft.com/topics/sex-in-heaven.htm.

Laaser, Mark. *Healing the Wounds of Sexual Addiction*. Grand Rapids: Zondervan, 2004.

Lewis, C. S. *Christian Reflections, Christianity and Culture*. Wheaton, IL: Tyndale, 1940.

———. *The Four Loves*. New York: Harcourt Brace Jovanovich, 1960.

Lincoln, Andrew T. *Ephesians*. Dallas: Word, 1990.

———. *The Gospel according to John*. New York: Continuum, 2005.

Linden, David J. *The Accidental Mind: How Brain Evolution Has Given Us Love, Memory, Dreams, and God*. Cambridge, Mass: Belknap, 2007.

Lutchmaya, Svetlana, and Simon Baron-Cohen. "Human Sex Differences in Social and Non-Social Looking Preferences at 12 Months of Age." *Infant Behavior & Development* 25 (2002): 319–25.

Lykken, David T. "The Causes and Costs of Crime and a Controversial Cure." *Journal of Personality* 68 (2000): 559–605.

Manning, Brennan. *Abba's Child*. Rev. ed. Colorado Springs: NavPress, 2002.

———. Brennan Manning's Official Home Page. www.brennanmanning.com.

———. *The Ragmuffin Gospel*. Sisters, OR: Multnomah, 1990.

Marazziti, D., et al. "Alteration of the Platelet Serotonin Transporter in Romantic Love." *Psychological Medicine* 29 (1999): 741–45.

Masters, William H., and Virginia E. Johnson. *Human Sexual Response*. Boston: Little, Brown, 1966.

McBride, Kimberly R., and J. Dennis Fortenberry. "Heterosexual Anal Sexuality and Anal Sex Behaviors: A Review." *Journal of Sex Research* 47 (2010): 123–36.

McCluskey, Christopher, and Rachel McCluskey. *When Two Become One: Enhancing Sexual Intimacy in Marriage*. Grand Rapids: Revell, 2004.

McKenzie-Mohr, Doug, and Mark P. Zanna. "Treating Women as Sexual Objects: Look to the (Gender Schematic) Male Who Has Viewed Pornography." *Personality and Social Psychology Bulletin* 16 (1990): 296–308.

McPherson, Miller, Lynn Smith-Lovin, and Matthew Brashears. "Social Isolation in America: Changes in Core Discussion Networks over Two Decades." *American Sociological Review* 71 (2006): 353–75.

McQuilkin, J. Robertson. "Living by Vows." *Christianity Today* 34.14 (Oct 8, 1990): 38–40.

———. "Muriel's Blessing." *Christianity Today* 40.2 (Feb. 5, 1996): 32–34.

Mehrabian, Albert, and Susan R. Ferris. "Inference of Attitudes from Nonverbal Communication in Two Channels." *Journal of Consulting Psychology* 31 (1967): 248–52.

Meltzer, Andrea L., and James K. McNulty. "Body Image and Marital Satisfaction: Evidence for the Mediating Role of Sexual Frequency and Sexual Satisfaction." *Journal of Family Psychology* 24 (2010): 156–64.

Meston, Cindy M., and David M. Buss. *Why Women Have Sex: Understanding Sexual Motivation—from Adventure to Revenge (and Everything in Between)*. New York: Time Books, 2009.

Meyer, Allan. *Search for Intimacy*. Victoria, Australia: Careforce Lifekeys, 2005.

Michael, Robert T., et al. *Sex in America: A Definitive Survey*. New York: Time Warner, 1995.

Middleton, J. Richard. *The Liberating Image: The* Imago Dei *in Genesis 1*. Grand Rapids: Brazos, 2005.

Miller, Calvin. *A Requiem for Love*. Dallas: Word, 1989.

Miller, Donald. *Blue Like Jazz: Nonreligious Thoughts on Christian Spirituality*. Nashville: Thomas Nelson, 2003.

Montagu, Ashley. *Touching: The Human Significance of Skin*. 3rd ed. New York: Harper, 1986.

Morris, Desmond. *Intimate Behaviour: A Sociologist's Classic Study of Human Intimacy*. New York: Kodansha International, 1997.

Mullins, Shawn. "Shimmer." EMI Blackwood Music and Roadieodie Music, 1998.

Newell, J. Philip. *Echo of the Soul: The Sacredness of the Human Body*. Harrisburg, PA: Morehouse, 2000.

Nouwen, Henri J. *The Return of the Prodigal Son: A Story of Homecoming*. New York: Doubleday, 1992.

Olds, Jacqueline, and Richard S. Schwartz. *The Lonely American: Drifting Apart in the Twenty-First Century*. Boston: Beacon Press, 2009.

Paul, Pamela. *Pornified: How Pornography Is Transforming Our Lives, Our Relationships, and Our Families*. New York: Henry Holt, 2005.

Penner, Clifford L., and Joyce J. Penner. *The Gift of Sex: A Guide to Sexual Fulfillment*. Nashville: W Publishing Group, 2003.

Perry, Bruce P., and R. Pollard. "Altered Brain Development Following Global Neglect in Early Childhood." Proceedings from the Annual Meeting of the Society for Neuroscience, New Orleans, 1997.

Piper, John. *Desiring God: Meditations of a Christian Hedonist*. Rev. ed. Colorado Springs: Multnomah Books, 2011.

Popenoe, David, and Barbara Dafoe Whitehead. *The State of Our Unions: The Social Health of Marriage in America 2007*. Piscataway, NJ: National Marriage Project, 2007. http://stateofourunions.org/pdfs/SOOU2007.pdf.

Prescott, J. W. "Body Pleasure and the Origins of Violence." *Bulletin of the Atomic Scientists* 11 (1975): 10–20.

———. "Early Somatosensory Deprivation as an Ontogenic Process in the Abnormal Development of Brain and Behavior." In *Medical Primatology*, edited by E. Goldsmith and J. Morr-Jankowski, 356–75. Basel, Switzerland: Karger, 1970.

Putnam, Robert. *Bowling Alone: The Collapse and Revival of American Community*. New York: Simon & Schuster, 2000.

Richard, Diane. "Christian Women Have More Fun." *Contemporary Sexuality* 34 (2000): 1–4.

Richards, Ramona. "Dirty Little Secret." *Today's Christian Woman* 25:5 (Sept/Oct 2003): 58.

Rinehart, Paula. *Sex and the Soul of a Woman*. Grand Rapids: Zondervan, 2004.

Risch, Gail S., Lisa A. Riley, and Michael G. Lawler. "Problematic Issues in the Early Years of Marriage: Content for Premarital Education." *Journal of Psychology and Theology* 21 (2003): 253–69.

Roberts, Barbara. *Not Under Bondage: Biblical Divorce for Abuse, Adultery, and Desertion*. Ballarat, Australia: Maschil, 2008.

Ropelato, Jerry. "Internet Pornography Statistics." http://internet-filter-review.topten reviews.com/internet-pornography-statistics.html.

Rosenau, Douglas E. *A Celebration of Sex: A Guide to Enjoying God's Gift of Sexual Intimacy*. Nashville: Thomas Nelson, 2002.

Russell, Diana. *Dangerous Relationships: Pornography, Misogyny, and Rape*. Thousand Oaks, CA: Sage, 1998.

Rymer, Russ. *Genie: A Scientific Tragedy*. San Francisco: HarperCollins, 1993.

Sarracino, Carmine, and Kevin M. Scott. *The Porning of America: The Rise of Porn Culture, What It Means, and Where We Go from Here*. Boston: Beacon Press, 2008.

Schneider, Jennifer P. "Effects of Cybersex Addiction on the Family: Results of a Survey." *Sexual Addiction & Compulsivity* 2 (2000): 31–58.

Schramm, David G., et al. "After 'I Do': The Newlywed Transition." *Marriage & Family Review* 38 (2005): 45–67.

Schwartz, Barry. *The Paradox of Choice: Why More Is Less*. New York: Harper Collins, 2004.

Shanor, Karen. *The Shanor Study: The Sexual Sensitivity of the American Male*. New York: Dial Press, 1978.

Shepherd, P. "Sex in Heaven?" *Expository Times* 104 (1993): 332–36.

Sherlock, Charles. *The Doctrine of Humanity*. Downers Grove, IL: InterVarsity, 1996.

Siegel, R. M., et al. "Screening for Domestic Violence in a Community Pediatric Setting." *Pediatrics* 104 (1999): 874–77.

Silverman, Jay G., et al. "Dating Violence against Adolescent Girls and Associated Substance Abuse, Unhealthy Weight Control, Sexual Risk Behavior, Pregnancy, and Suicidality." *Journal of the American Medical Association* 286 (2001): 572–79.

Smedes, Lewis B. *Forgive and Forget: Healing the Hurts We Don't Deserve*. Rev. ed. San Francisco: HarperCollins, 1996.

———. *Sex for Christians: The Limits and Liberties of Sexual Living*. Grand Rapids: Eerdmans, 1976.

Smith, S. M. "Perichoresis." *Evangelical Dictionary of Theology.* Grand Rapids: Baker, 1990.

Spencer, William and Aida, Steve and Celestia Tracy. *Marriage at the Crossroads: Couples in Conversation about Discipleship, Gender Roles, Decision-Making, and Intimacy.* Downers Grove, IL: InterVarsity, 2009.

Stepp, Laura Session. *Unhooked: How Young Women Pursue Sex, Delay Love, and Lose at Both.* New York: Riverhead Books, 2007.

Straus, Jillian. *Unhooked Generation: The Truth About Why We're Still Single.* New York: Hyperion, 2006.

Teicher, Martin H., et al. "Childhood Neglect Is Associated with Reduced Corpus Callosum Area." *Biological Psychiatry* 56 (2004): 80–85.

Thomas, Gary. *Sacred Marriage: What if God Designed Marriage to Make Us Holy More than to Make Us Happy?* Grand Rapids: Zondervan, 2000.

Tjaden, P., and N. Thoennes. *Prevalence, Incidence, and Consequences of Violence against Women: Findings from the National Violence against Women Survey.* Washington D.C.: U.S. Department of Justice, 1998.

Torrence, T. F. *The Christian Doctrine of God: One Being, Three Persons.* London: T. & T. Clark, 1996.

Tracy, Steven R. "Chastity and the Goodness of God: The Case for Premarital Abstinence." *Themelios* 31 (2006): 54–71.

———. *Mending the Soul: Understanding and Healing Abuse.* Grand Rapids: Zondervan, 2005.

Treas, Judith, and Deirdre Giesen. "Sexual Infidelity among Married and Cohabiting Couples." *Journal of Marriage and the Family* 62 (2000): 48–60.

Trobisch, Walter. *I Loved a Girl.* New York: Harper & Row, 1975.

Turpin, Adrian. "Not tonight darling, I'm online." Financial Times.com, March 31, 2006.

Twenge, Jean, et al. "Egos Inflating Over Time: A Cross-Temporal Meta-Analysis of the Narcissistic Personality Inventory." *Journal of Personality* 76 (2008): 875–901.

Twenge, Jean M., and W. Keith Campbell. *The Narcissism Epidemic: Living in the Age of Entitlement.* New York: Free Press, 2009.

Vanauken, Sheldon. *A Severe Mercy.* New York: Harper & Row, 1977.

Waite, Linda J., and Maggie Gallagher. *The Case for Marriage: Why Married People Are Happier, Healthier, and Better Off Financially.* New York: Broadway Books, 2000.

Waite, Linda J., and Kara Joyner. "Emotional and Physical Satisfaction with Sex in Married, Cohabiting, and Dating Sexual Unions: Do Men and Women Differ?" In *Sex, Love, and Health in America: Private Choices and Public Policies,* edited by Edward O. Laumann and Robert T. Michael, 239–69. Chicago: University of Chicago Press, 2001.

Wangerin, Walter. *As for Me and My House: Crafting Your Marriage to Last.* Rev. ed. Nashville: Thomas Nelson, 1990.

———. "Edification/Demolition." In *Ragman and Other Cries of Faith,* 178–81. New York: HarperCollins, 1984.

Weingarten, Gene. "Pearls Before Breakfast." *The Washington Post,* April 8, 2007. http://www.washingtonpost.com/wp-dyn/content/article/2007/04/04/AR2007040401721.html.

Wenham, Gordon J. "Family in the Pentateuch." In *Family in the Bible: Exploring Customs, Culture, and Context,* edited by Richard S. Hess and M. Daniel Carroll, 17–31. Grand Rapids: Baker, 2003.

————. *Genesis 1–15*. Waco, TX: Word, 1987.

Wilson, Sandra D. *Into Abba's Arms: Finding the Acceptance You've Always Wanted.* Wheaton, IL: Tyndale, 1998.

Yancey, Philip D. *What's So Amazing about Grace?* Grand Rapids: Zondervan, 1997.

Young, Michael, et al. "Sexual Satisfaction among Married Women." *American Journal of Health Studies* 16 (2000): 73–85.

Zak, Paul J., Angela A. Stanton, and Sheila Ahmadi. "Oxytocin Increases Generosity in Humans." *PLoS ONE* 2(11): e1128. http://www.plosone.org/article/info%3Adoi %2F10.1371%2Fjournal.pone.0001128.

Zillmann, Dolf. "Effects of Prolonged Consumption of Pornography." In *Pornography Research Advances and Policy Considerations,* edited by Dolf Zillmann and Jennings Bryant, 125–57. Hillsdale, NJ: Lawrence Erlbaum, 1989.

Zillmann, Dolf, and Jennings Bryant. "Pornography, Sexual Callousness, and the Trivialization of Rape." *Journal of Communication* 32 (1982): 10–21.

————. "Pornography's Impact on Sexual Satisfaction." *Journal of Applied Social Psychology* 18 (1988): 438–53.

Ziziouslas, John. *Being as Communion: Studies in Personhood and the Church.* Crestwood, NY: St. Vladimir's Seminary Press, 1985.

Scripture Index

190 Scripture Index

Job (cont.)

| 21:2 | 74 |
| 24:7 | 10 |

Psalms

21:6	68
139	72
139:13–14	143
139:13–16	85

Proverbs

2:16–22	102
4:20	74
5:3–20	102
5:18–19	141
6:20–35	102
7:5–25	102
12:18	74
17:27–28	74
18:13–15	74
19:14	82, 143
20:5	74
22:14	102
23:12	74
29:19	74
31:10–12	96
31:26–30	96

Ecclesiastes

4:9–10	xii
4:12	xii
10:12–14	74
11:5	85

Song of Songs

1:2	133, 142
1:2–4	118
1:15–16	162
1:15–17	165
4:1–7	131, 146, 151
4:16	152
5:1	135
5:9–16	451
5:9—6:01	95
6:3	116
7:6–10	141

| 7:12–14 | 160 |
| 8:6–7 | 121 |

Isaiah

| 55:1–5 | 83 |

Ezekiel

| 18:16 | 10 |
| 36:26 | 67 |

Daniel

| 3:1 | 8 |
| 10:16 | 8 |

Hosea

2	164
2:3	10
2:14–20	xiv
10:12	55

Matthew

3:16–17	11
5:27–28	142
5:28	38
8:1–3	114
8:5–13	114
12:17–21	11
17:5	11
19:15	114
20:32–34	114
26:48	114

Mark

6:5	114
8:22–23	114
10:13–16	114

Luke

1:50	90
2:19	74
6:19	114
8:18	74
8:42–48	114
8:54	114
14:26	98
15:20	115

Subject Index